Warman's

Vintage Jewelry

IDENTIFICATION AND PRICE GUIDE

LEIGH LESHNER

Published by

krause publications

An Imprint of F+W Publications

700 East State Street • Iola, WI 54990-0001
715-445-2214 • 888-457-2873
www.krausebooks.com

Our toll-free number to place an order or obtain
a free catalog is (800) 258-0929.

Library of Congress Control Number: 2007942607

ISBN-13: 978-0-89689-639-0
ISBN-10: 0-89689-639-0

Designed by Marilyn McGrane
Edited by Mary Sieber

Printed in Singapore

OTHER JEWELRY BOOKS BY KRAUSE PUBLICATIONS

Antique Trader Jewelry Price Guide by Kyle Husfloen

Collecting Art Plastic Jewelry by Leigh Leshner

Collecting Victorian Jewelry by C. Jeanenne Bell

Costume Jewelry Identification and Price Guide by Leigh Leshner

Rhinestone Jewelry Identification and Price Guide by Leigh Leshner

Secrets to Collecting Jewelry by Leigh Leshner

Costume Jewelry Figurals Identification and Price Guide by Kathy Flood

Warman's Jewelry Identification and Price Guide by Christie Romero

Warman's Jewelry Field Guide by Leigh Leshner

Acknowledgments

I wish to thank my parents, Robert and Carol Leshner, and my sister, Michelle, for their encouragement and continued support.

Maurice Childs for his extraordinary photography.

My editor Mary Sieber, designer Marilyn McGrane, and editorial director Paul Kennedy.

Contents

Introduction

At a very young age, I fell in love with antique and vintage jewelry. The 1920s through the 1940s gave us wonderful pieces of jewelry made of all types of white metal and rhinestones. It is a world within itself, full of history, beauty, and mystery.

Costume jewelry is reflective of the times as well as social and aesthetic movements. Each piece tells its own story through hidden clues that, when interpreted, will help solve the mysteries surrounding them. The jewelry is at times rich and elegant and at other times ornate yet simple. The pieces range in size and vary from delicate to bold. Whether you are looking for elaborate pieces or simple beauty, you are able to find it in the jewelry made during this time period.

As a collector, dealer, or someone who has inherited a piece of old jewelry, you may have several questions that you want answered. What it is made of, what is the history behind the piece, how old is it, and the most common question—what is it worth? By providing examples and historical information, this book will answer these often asked questions.

Collecting Vintage Jewelry

Boucher double bird brooch, rhodium and clear and red rhinestones, faux pearls, **$225**.

Double bird brooch, pot metal and clear and pink rhinestones, faux pearls, enameling, **$185**.

When you are collecting vintage jewelry, you need to focus on several things: condition, price, quality, scarcity/rarity, age, and design. Is the piece well made? Is it missing any stones or pieces? Can the piece be repaired, and how much will the repair cost? Are the stones hand set? Is the piece stamped or cast? These are all questions that you need to ask yourself when you are purchasing a piece of jewelry.

To do this, one of the most important tools that you need is a loupe. A loupe is an instrument that allows you to see detail in the jewelry. It magnifies the object that you are looking at. Loupes come in varying sizes and magnifications. The average magnification level that most people use is a 10X, which means that the magnification will be ten times the actual size. To use the loupe, hold it about an inch away from your eye, and then bring the object that you want to look at up to the loupe until you see it in focus. Be sure to keep both eyes open to view the item.

- Condition is first and foremost. Don't overlook this. Be conscious of the condition of the piece because it will affect its value.
- Price is always a consideration, but the first rule of collecting is to collect what you like! Don't worry about trends or what's the hot new collectible. Focus on amassing a collection that makes you smile, that intrigues you, that inspires you. Whatever type of jewelry you buy, buy what you like, and buy the best examples of what you like that you can afford.
- The quality of the piece is also important. Look at the design of the piece. Is it intricate and ornate? Is it handmade or machine made? How is the finish on the piece? The more detail that is involved and the more handwork that is involved will generally make a piece of jewelry more valuable.
- While age does play a role in the value of a piece, don't be fooled into believing that antique jewelry has to be more than 100 years old to have any value, and that the older the piece the more valuable it is regardless of the condition.
- The factor of the design of the piece is a more subjective personal evaluation. It has more to do with your own personal taste. However, the design of the piece can help you determine its age and identify the period and style.
- Scarcity and rarity play a role in the price of a piece. Obviously, if a piece of jewelry is rare and hard to find, the price will reflect it. But if a dealer has multiples of the same piece, be wary. These items can be old store stock or reproductions. In either case, when multiples are available, the price should not be high.

Double bird brooch, pot metal and clear rhinestones, faux pearls, enameling, **$165**.

White Metal and Rhinestone Jewelry 1920s, 1930s, and 1940s

Costume jewelry was an outgrowth of the desire of the average person to have copies of gemstone and precious metal jewelry that had previously been reserved for the wealthy. Costume jewelry began its steady ascent to popularity in the 1920s. Since it was relatively inexpensive to produce, there was mass production. The sizes and designs of the jewelry varied. Often, it was worn a few times, disposed of and then replaced with a new piece. It was thought of as expendable—a cheap throwaway to dress up an outfit. Costume jewelry became so popular that it was sold in upscale stores as well as the five-and-dime.

Even though the cost was relatively low, each piece brought pleasure to its wearer. The designs had an intrinsic beauty that made them unique and special. The designs ranged from the subtle to the outrageous. Because of the relatively inexpensive production costs, designers were able to unleash their creativity while at the same time maintain high production standards. Many of the designers had backgrounds in fine jewelry, and they brought their knowledge and skill to this new phenomena of "fake" jewelry. These were jewelers who were used to working with gemstones. They now were able to take their glorious designs and interpret them into costume jewelry for the average woman. The quality was unsurpassed, and the designs were unique and often rivaled their "real" counterparts.

While many pieces of jewelry were made by well-recognized designers and companies, a greater percentage of the jewelry was unsigned. These signed as well as unsigned pieces were works of art. The designers were free to express themselves in an unbridled fashion that was evident in the designs that ranged from whimsical to elegant. Just as with any other item, there was a wide range of quality in terms of the materials that were used. Pieces ranged from low-end base metal to higher-end sterling. While the materials may have been different in terms of perceived quality, the finished product was a sight to behold. The designs included flowers, figurals, bows, Art Deco designs, animals, geometric designs, and much more. The designers not only used rhinestones to enhance the metal, but they incorporated molded glass, beads, faux pearls, and semi-precious stones. Enameling techniques were often used to add color. (See photographs 1 and 2.)

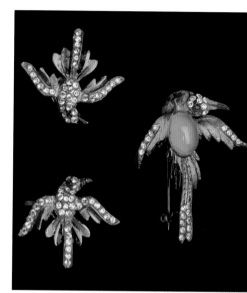

Photo 2: Bird pin and matching earrings, pot metal and clear and red rhinestones, blue glass cabochon, enameling, **$165.**

Photo 1: From left: flower brooch, pot metal and clear rhinestones, enameling, **$145;** flower brooch, pot metal and clear rhinestones, enameling, some wear to enamel, **$125;** double flower brooch, pot metal and clear rhinestones, enameling, some wear to the enamel, **$120.**

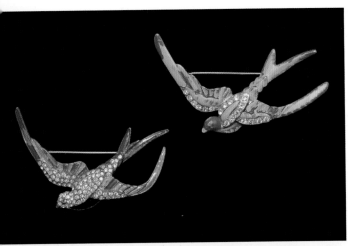

Photo 3: From left: bird brooch, pot metal and clear and blue rhinestones, enameling, some wear to enamel, **$110**; bird brooch, pot metal and clear rhinestones, enameling, **$95**.

Photo 4: From left: bow brooch, pot metal and clear rhinestones, black paint, **$62**; bow Brooch, pot metal and clear rhinestones, black enameling, **$98**.

Photo 5: Coro dog brooches: pot metal and clear rhinestones, tan molded glass, **$165**; pot metal and clear rhinestones, blue molded glass, **$185**.

During the 1920s, the fashion of the times was changing. World War I had an effect on clothing designs. The style went from tight, narrow, floor-length skirts to fuller, shorter hemlines. Curves had been abandoned in favor of more loose fitting drop-waisted dresses. There were two distinct styles of the '20s: the feminine style and the androgynous style often referred to as the jeune fille look. This style emphasized a modern look for the time, which was a loose, straight cut de-emphasizing the hourglass figure of a woman's body. The clothing had become lighter and more ornate. Dresses were accented with beads and fringe. Women began bobbing their hair, which led to the adornment of chandelier-type earrings. Low cut dress lines were accompanied by sautoirs, flapper beads, and chokers that drew attention to the décolletage. This also led to women wearing delicate chokers and pendants as well as multiple bracelets. Furs and boas adorned with fur clips and bold brooches were also popular.

The 1920s featured an overlap of styles consisting of Edwardian, Art Nouveau, and Art Deco. Many jewelry pieces incorporated the graceful and naturalistic curving Art Nouveau styles while others had an Edwardian look that imitated the platinum and diamonds that were prevalent of this style. These designs were imitations made to look like their real counterparts.

The predominant style of the times was Art Deco. The designs were geometric and bold. They were streamlined, stylized, and angular. Fashions were often accompanied by jewelry that drew on the Art Deco movement. The Art Deco movement, 1920-1935, began in Paris at the Exposition Internationale des Arts Decoratifs et Industriels Modernes. The idea behind this movement was that form follows function. The style was characterized by simple, straight clean lines, stylized motifs, geometric shapes, and streamlined curves. Zigzag designs and sharp angles accented by colored stones and strong contrasting colors were in vogue.

One designer who played an important role not only in clothing design but also in costume jewelry design was Coco Chanel. She created costume jewelry to decorate her clothing. She knew the true meaning of the complete costume, and she began wearing her costume jewelry; jewelry generally reserved for evening wear, but Chanel wore it during the day, making it fashionable for millions of other women to do so, too.

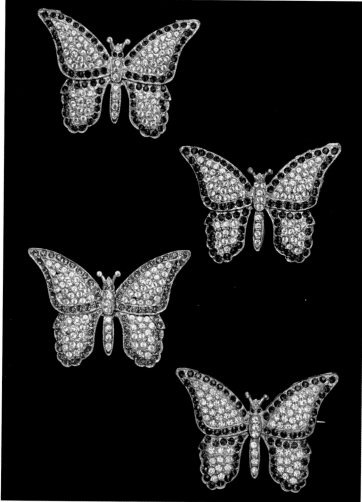

Photo 6: From top: butterfly brooch, pot metal and clear and red rhinestones, **$110**; butterfly brooch, pot metal and green and clear rhinestones, **$110**; butterfly brooch, pot metal and clear and blue rhinestones, **$110**; butterfly brooch, pot metal and clear and purple rhinestones, **$110**.

Photo 7: From top: butterfly brooch, pot metal and clear and green rhinestones, clear faceted glass, **$285**; butterfly brooch, pot metal and clear and blue rhinestones, blue faceted glass, **$285**.

For the most part, the 1920s was known as the "White Period." This referred to the prevalent use of clear rhinestones set in white metal. Gradually, the jewelry moved toward bolder colors. White metal was accented with dramatic colored stones in ruby, sapphire, emerald, black, amethyst, and topaz.

At times there were variations of the same designs that were interpreted differently by each designer. (See photographs 3 and 4.)

Sometimes, these variations were created within the same company's designs of a particular piece of jewelry. (See photograph 5.)

Other times, manufacturers would create the casts for brooches and designers and companies would purchase the unfinished pieces and then set the stones in various color schemes. (See photographs 6 and 7.)

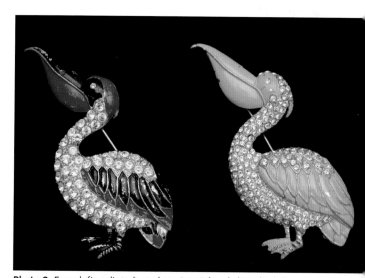

Photo 8: From left: pelican brooch, pot metal and clear rhinestones, enameling, wear to enamel, **$295**; pelican brooch, pot metal and clear rhinestones, enameling, wear to enamel, **$295**.

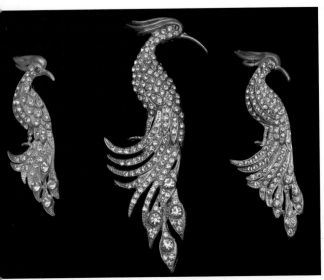

Photo 9: Bird brooches, pot metal and clear rhinestones, from left: **$110, $185, and $135**.

Photo 10: Fish brooches, pot metal and clear rhinestones, enameling, from top left clockwise: **$110, $95, and $125**.

Photo 11: From left: bird brooch, pot metal and clear and red rhinestones, **$145**; bird brooch, sterling and clear rhinestones, **$165**; bird brooch, pot metal and clear and red rhinestones, **$145**.

Designers used different color enameling as well. (See photograph 8.)

It was also commonplace to have the same design in varying sizes. (See photographs 9 and 10.)

The same brooch was also made using different materials such as pot metal and sterling. (See photograph 11.)

The 1930s was considerably quieter than the 1920s. With the Depression and the advent of World War II, times were changing. These world changes affected society as a whole. Labor-intensive fashion was no longer economically viable. The designs began to move back to a more sculptured, softer, feminine look. Clothing was now functional and meant to last a long time. The lines were softened. Jewelry was a bit simpler than in the 1920s, though not too simplistic. While life was in turmoil, jewelry now provided a respite. Women could purchase a relatively inexpensive piece of jewelry to spruce up an old outfit and make it look new. Designers began using enameling and brightly colored rhinestones to create wonderful whimsical designs of birds, flowers, circus animals, bows, dogs, and just about every other figural you can imagine. The jewelry was bright and festive. The white metal was often dipped in a gold wash to add color. (See photographs 12 and 13.)

The 1940s took the designs to bigger and bolder heights. Jewelry had a more substantial feel to it, and many designers began using larger stones to enhance the dramatic pieces. Common themes running throughout the designs were bows, flowers, and sunbursts. Reflecting the mood of the country, clothing had a very militaristic feel to it. The predominant materials used were rayon, wool, and linen. The clothing had big boxy

Photo 12: Floral brooch, pot metal with a gold wash, clear rhinestones, faux pearls, and enameling, **$165**.

Photo 13: Lily brooch, pot metal with gold wash, clear rhinestones, orange glass beads, and enameling, **$125**.

Photo 14: From top: lily trembler brooch, pot metal and clear rhinestones, **$155**; lily trembler brooch, pot metal and clear and blue rhinestones, **$155**.

shoulders, slim skirts accented by stockings and high heels. Again, fur was very much in style, and large bold fur clips often adorned it.

Because of World War II, the use of pot metal, specifically the tin and lead used in pot metal, was prohibited for use other than for the military. Sterling now became the metal of necessity. Patriotism was also running high, and sweetheart jewelry became fashionable. This jewelry was made and worn as a sign of the support for the war effort and as sentimental treasures for those who were fighting the war. Common themes of this jewelry were American flags, a V-sign for victory, Uncle Sam's hat, airplanes, anchors, and eagles.

The designers' creations using white metal and rhinestones were unlimited. They began using spring mechanisms to create jewelry that moved, called tremblers. Parts of the jewelry, such as the stamen of a flower, would be attached to a small coiled piece of wire that allowed it to move as the wearer moved. (See photographs 14 and 15.)

Jewelry was also created that had moving parts such as the bell and the ribbons on these brooches. (See photographs 16 and 17.)

Photo 16: Lantern brooch, lantern moves, rhodium and clear and green rhinestones, **$125**.

Photo 17: Art Deco bow brooch, rhodium and clear rhinestones, green faceted glass, **$185**.

Photo 15: Lily brooch and matching earrings, trembler, pot metal and clear rhinestones, **$255**.

11

Photo 18: The front of a dress clip.

Photo 19: The back of a dress clip.

Photo 20: Back view of a fur clip. Note the thin prongs.

Jewelry was also functional. Dress clips were especially popular in the 1930s. Dress clips have a flat-hinged clip with prongs that grasp the fabric to hold the clip in place. (See photographs 18 and 19.)

Fur clips were popular in the 1940s and can be distinguished from dress clips because the prongs on the back are two thin prongs with a sharp tip. (See photograph 20.)

In 1931 Coro patented the Duette, and in 1936 Trifari patented the Clipmate. Both of these creations were brooches that consisted of two dress clips or fur clips that could come apart from the pin and be worn separately or as one large brooch. (See photographs 21, 22, 23, 24, 25, and 26.)

Photos 21 and 22: Rhinestone Coro Duette with dress clips.

Clothing became the background to showcase beautiful designs. Women began wearing dress clips and pins on hats. Belts were adorned with rhinestone buckles and brooches. Dress clips were worn in the V of a neckline or in the square of a neckline.

Dress clips were prevalent during this period, so they are readily available and easily found. However, they are often overlooked because people don't know how to wear them. Dress clips can be worn in many ways. They can be worn in the traditional manner in the V of a neckline or the square of the neckline. They can be slipped over a cord or chain and worn as a necklace. They can be clipped onto a pocket or placed on a sleeve that has been rolled up. Hats can be adorned with them. They can also be converted into a brooch by placing a safety pin inside a shirt or jacket so that the pin bar goes through the material, then simply drop the clip over the bar and you now have a brooch.

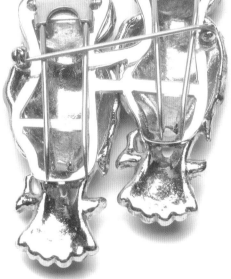

Photos 23 and 24: Coro Duette with fur clips.

Photos 25 and 26: Example of a Trifari Clipmate.

The History of Rhinestones

Czechoslovakian glass or Bohemian glass as it was originally known had its beginnings in the 13th and 14th centuries in Bohemia, a part of the Czech Republic. The country has a history rich in glassmaking, including hand blown, molded, and cut glass. The introduction of lead compounds is responsible for the clarity and brilliance of the glass and is known as lead crystal. The center of Czechoslovakian jewelry production was Gablonz, where there had always been a tradition of glassmaking.

Glass was not limited to functional objects. By 1918, the Czechoslovakian glass industry began to use innovative and creative techniques and incorporated them in jewelry designs. Thousands of people worked out of their homes as glass pressers, grinders, and cutters to make perfume bottles, vanity items, beads, and rhinestones.

Rhinestones were manmade gemstones from highly refined glass. The glass is first colored the desired color by the introduction of various metals, and then it is pressed into molds to create the final shape. Each stone is ground and polished on all facets by machine to extract the brilliance. The stones are generally foiled. This opaque back coating increases the reflectivity and brilliance while allowing the back of the stone to be glued into the setting without seeing the glue. (See photograph at left.)

Rhinestones are often referred to as "paste." Originally, glass paste was glass that was ground into a paste, molded then melted. The final piece was an opaque, dense glass with a frosted surface. The paste would have numerous air bubbles and swirl marks, but the highly leaded glass was cut with facets to reflect the light, and it was backed by a copper or silver lining.

When the term "paste" is currently used, it generally refers to rhinestones. While the United States uses the term "rhinestone," the terms "paste," "strass," and "diamente" are often used in Europe.

The term "rhinestone" came from the Rhine River in Austria. The river in the late 1800s was filled with quartz pebbles in brilliant colors. As this source was depleted, imitation glass rhinestones replaced them.

Another region that was responsible for the creation of the rhinestone was Austria. In 1891, Daniel Swarovski revolutionized the jewelry business when he created a new glass-cutting machine that could mechanically cut faceted glass. Previously, it would take long periods of time to finish stones by hand. Now, stones could be created in a fraction of the time.

Swarovski had a background in glassmaking, and he soon began making rhinestones with a 32% high lead content that produced faceted stones with refractions unrivaled by any other company. He also revolutionized the rhinestone business by creating vacuum plating with silver and gold for the backs of the stones. By doing this, he again reduced the need for hand labor.

Because of Daniel Swarovski's efforts, ingenuity, and imagination, Swarovski stones are considered the highest quality rhinestones and are used by more than 85% of the American jewelry companies.

Settings

Several different types of settings are used for the rhinestones:

BEAD SET: *Small burrs of metal rise out of the base of the pin to hold the individual rhinestones in place.*

BEZEL SET: *The stone is held in place by a band of metal that is placed around the outside of each stone. This is a time-consuming and expensive method.*

CHANNEL SET: *The rhinestones rest in a metal channel and are held in place only by a slight rim that runs along the edge of the channel. In this method, the stones are set side-by-side so no metal is seen between the stones.*

HAND SET: *Stones are glued in individually in a scooped out cup in the metal.*

HAND SET WITH METAL PRONGS: *Stones are hand set and then the metal prongs are bent over the top of the stone.*

PAVÉ SET: *Occurs when the stones are set together in a group so that the underlying metal surface is hidden.*

PRONG SET: *Stones are set and then metal prongs are bent over the top of the stones by a machine.*

Cuts and Shapes of Rhinestones

Rhinestones are both affordable and fashionable. They come in many shapes and sizes. The various cuts are:

BAGUETTE: *A narrow, elongated, rectangular-shaped, faceted stone.*

CABOCHON: *A round, dome-shaped stone having a flat back. They are usually opaque or translucent, but can have a foiled back.*

CHATON: *A stone that has eight facets on top and eight facets on the bottom. The top is flat and the bottom comes to a point. There are several parts of a chaton. The flat top is known as a table. The girdle is the place where the top and the bottom of the stone meet. The crown is the part of the stone that is above the girdle. The pavilion is the bottom part of the stone under the girdle. The culet is the point of the stone.*

DENTELLES: *A stone that is formed in a mold and then hand cut. There are either 18, 32, or 64 facets on the back and front of the stone. Light is refracted through the facets in the stone's surface.*

UNFOILED DENTELLES: *A large glass stone that is molded and then hand cut to add facets. The light is refracted through the faceted cuts on the glass. There is no backing on the glass. This stone was popular in the 1920s through the 1940s.*

EMERALD CUT: *A square cut stone with faceted edges.*

Back view   *Front view*

FLAT BACK RHINESTONE: *The top of the stone is faceted and the back is flat.*

MARQUISE: *A faceted stone that is oval-shaped with a point on each side of the stone, and a flat top.*

OVAL: *an oval-shaped rhinestone with faceted edges.*

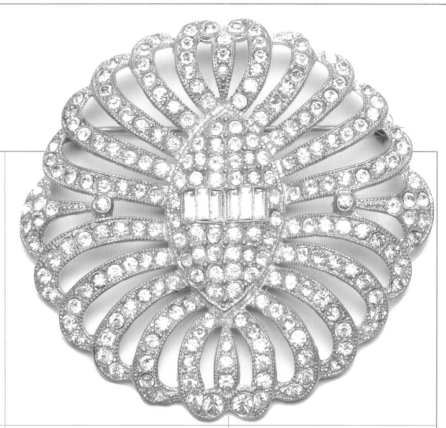

PEAR CUT: *A faceted, teardrop-shaped stone.*

POINT BACK: *A rhinestone that has a back that culminates in a point.*

ROUND CUT: *A round-shaped stone with faceted edges.*

SQUARE CUT: *A square-shaped stone with faceted edges.*

TRIANGULAR CUT: *A triangular-cut, faceted stone based on a brilliant-cut style.*

NOT PICTURED:

MINE CUT: *A square stone with rounded corners, sometimes called a cushion shape. Thirty-two crown facets and 24 pavilion facets with a table and culet.*

PRINCESS CUT: *A faceted square-cut stone, sometimes now known as a quadrillium or squarillion cut.*

ROSE CUT: *A flat-base stone with 24 triangular facets meeting at the top in a point.*

PLEASE NOTE: *Mine cut, princess cut, and rose cut are types of cuts that are generally used for real gemstones, though some have been used for gemstones such as garnets, and on very rare occasions for rhinestones. I've included them above because the terms are often bandied about, but collectors should be aware that these cuts are rarely used for rhinestones.*

Care of Costume Jewelry

Art Deco brooch, pot metal and clear rhinestones, clear faceted glass, **$245**.

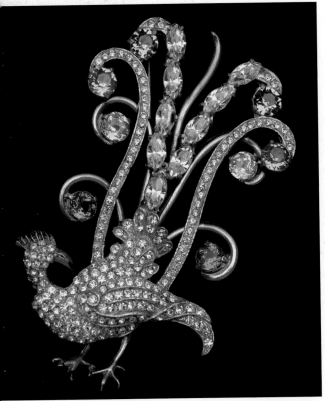

Peacock brooch, pot metal and clear, pink, blue, green, and citrine rhinestones, **$265**.

• Do not spray perfumes, deodorants, or hairsprays around rhinestone jewelry. The products will adhere to the stones and will cause damage to them.

• Do not store rhinestone jewelry in plastic bags for prolonged periods of time. Moisture will be trapped inside, destroying the rhinestones.

• Do not store rhinestone jewelry in hot areas or in direct sunlight. The heat will cause the glue to melt and can also cause moisture to form, which will destroy the rhinestones.

• Do not store pieces of rhinestone jewelry on top of one another. The rhinestones are made from glass and can chip or crack.

• Pot metal is a soft material. Care must be taken not bend or crush it.

• It is important to remember that a rhinestone has a foil back, which will become damaged when it is exposed to moisture. Never dip rhinestone jewelry in any kind of liquid. This will damage the piece. If you need to clean rhinestone jewelry, spread out a towel and lay the piece on the towel. Then using a clean, dry cosmetic brush, dust the piece off. If the stones seem cloudy, you can clean them with a glass cleaner. To do this, dip a toothbrush into the cleaner and then tap off the excess liquid. Then brush the stones gently, taking care not to get the liquid into the setting as it will destroy the foil backing and the rhinestone will lose its brilliance. After you have finished brushing the piece, turn it upside down onto the towel and let it dry for three to four hours before you put it away.

Art Deco brooch, pot metal and clear rhinestones, clear faceted glass, **$325**.

Price Guide

Values in the price guide are only a guide. Values vary according to each piece of jewelry's condition, quality, design, and/or the geographic location where the piece is purchased.

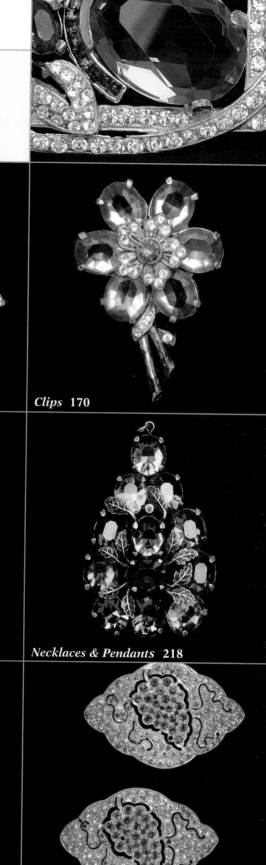

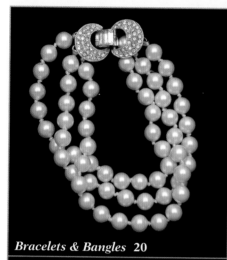

Bracelets & Bangles 20

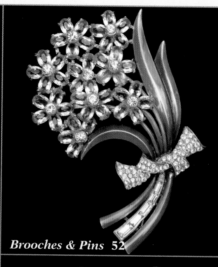

Brooches & Pins 52

Clips 170

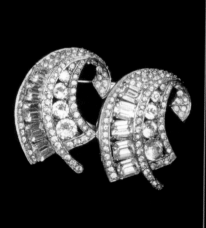

Duettes 202

Earrings 206

Necklaces & Pendants 218

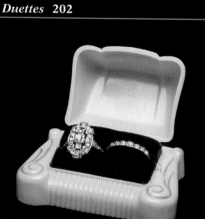

Rings 238

Sets 242

Miscellaneous 250

Bracelets & Bangles

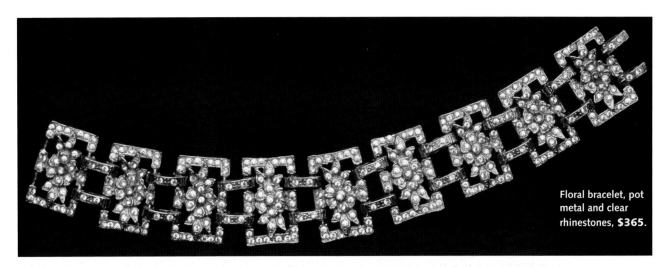

Floral bracelet, pot metal and clear rhinestones, **$365**.

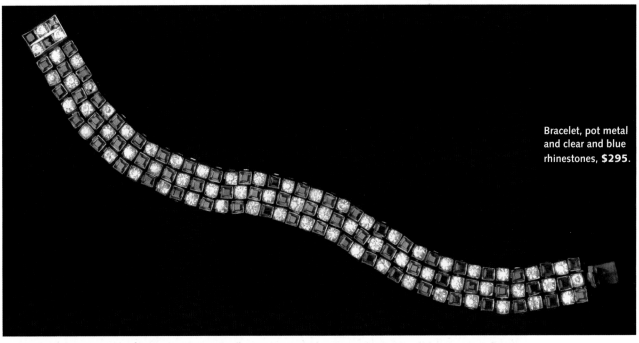

Bracelet, pot metal and clear and blue rhinestones, **$295**.

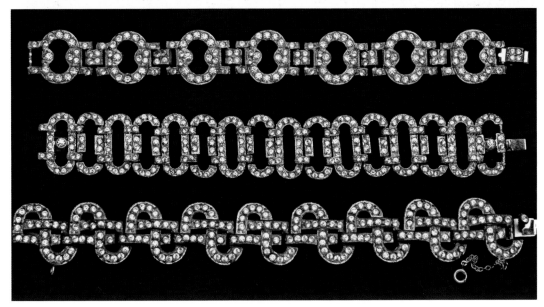

From top: Art Deco bracelet, pot metal and clear rhinestones, **$195**; Art Deco bracelet, rhodium and clear rhinestones, **$245**; Art Deco bracelet, pot metal and clear rhinestones, **$198**.

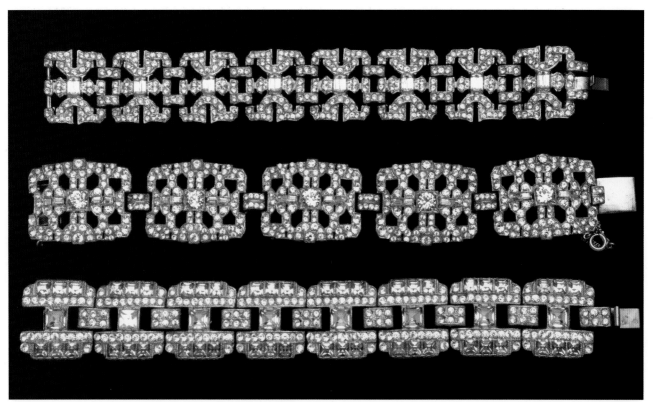

From top: Art Deco bracelet, rhodium and clear rhinestones, **$425**; Art Deco bracelet, rhodium and clear rhinestones, **$495**; Art Deco bracelet, pot metal and clear rhinestones, **$395**.

From top: Art Deco bracelet, rhodium and clear rhinestones, **$285**; Art Deco bracelet, rhodium and clear rhinestones, **$395**; Art Deco bracelet, pot metal and clear rhinestones, **$295**; bow design bracelet, rhodium and clear rhinestones, **$245**.

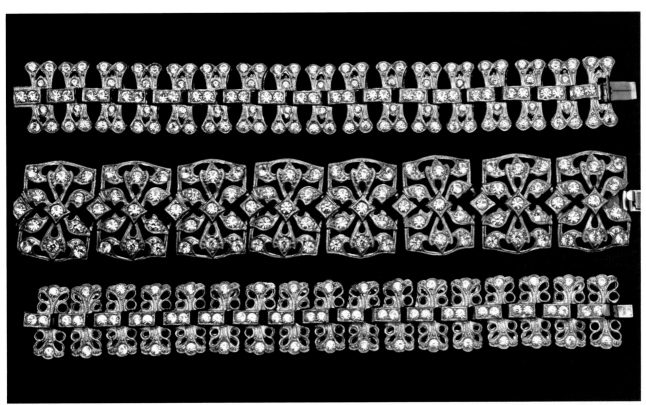

From top: Art Deco bracelet, pot metal and clear rhinestones, **$165**; bracelet, pot metal and clear rhinestones, **$145**; bracelet, pot metal and clear rhinestones, **$148**.

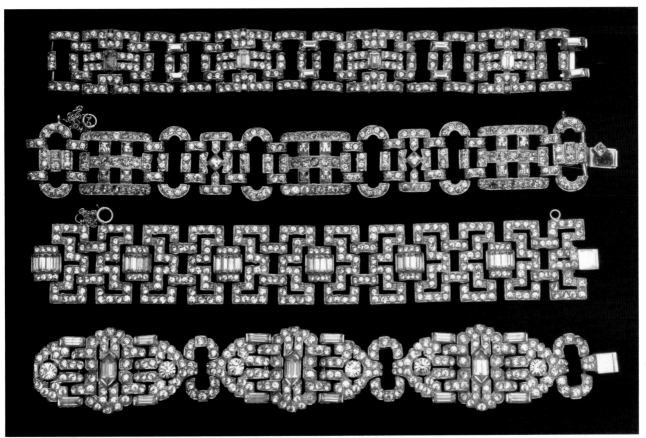

From top: Art Deco bracelet, pot metal and clear rhinestones, **$325**; Art Deco bracelet, pot metal and clear rhinestones, **$325**; Art Deco bracelet, rhodium and clear rhinestones, **$425**; Art Deco bracelet, rhodium and clear rhinestones, **$395**.

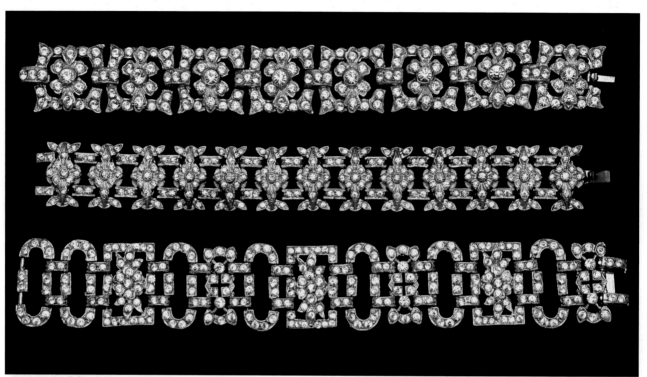

From top: floral design bracelet, pot metal and clear rhinestones, **$185**; floral design bracelet, rhodium and clear rhinestones, **$245**; floral design bracelet, rhodium and clear rhinestones, **$425**.

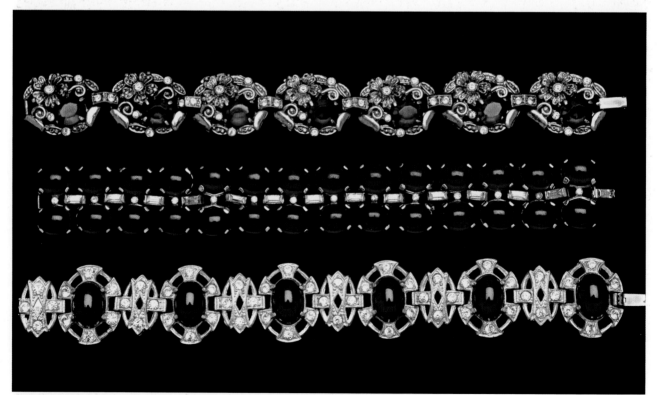

From top: floral design bracelet, pot metal and clear and green rhinestones, **$165**; Trifari bracelet, pot metal and clear rhinestones, green glass cabochons, **$195**; Art Deco bracelet, pot metal and clear rhinestones, green glass cabochons, **$135**.

From top: bracelet, sterling and clear rhinestones, faux pearls, **$195**; Otis bracelet, sterling and clear rhinestones, **$345**; buckle bracelet, sterling and clear rhinestones, **$295**.

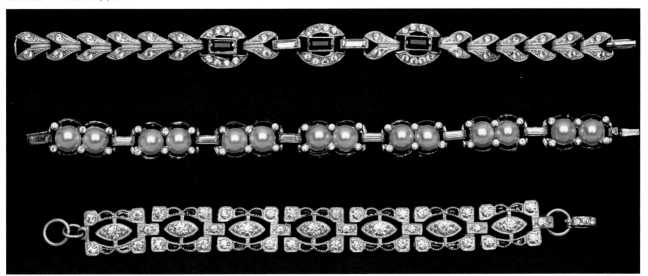

From top: Art Deco bracelet, pot metal and clear and black rhinestones, **$115**; Art Deco bracelet, enameling, pot metal and clear rhinestones, faux pearls, **$115**; Art Deco bracelet, enameling, pot metal and clear rhinestones, **$95**.

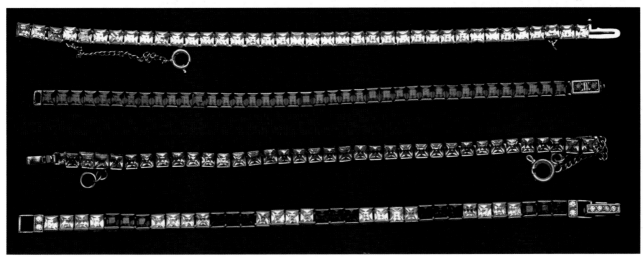

From top: line bracelet, rhodium and clear rhinestones, **$75**; line bracelet, sterling and red rhinestones, **$135**; line bracelet, rhodium and light blue rhinestones, **$80**; Otis line bracelet, sterling and clear and blue rhinestones, **$135**.

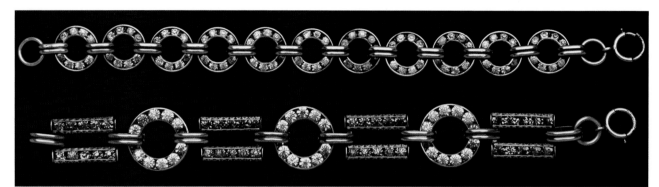

From top: Art Deco bracelet, sterling and clear rhinestones, **$195**; Art Deco bracelet, sterling and clear and blue rhinestones, **$285**.

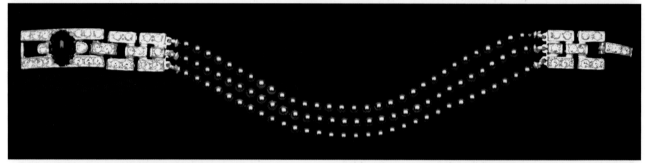

Bracelet, pot metal and clear rhinestones, black glass cabochon and black beads, **$125**.

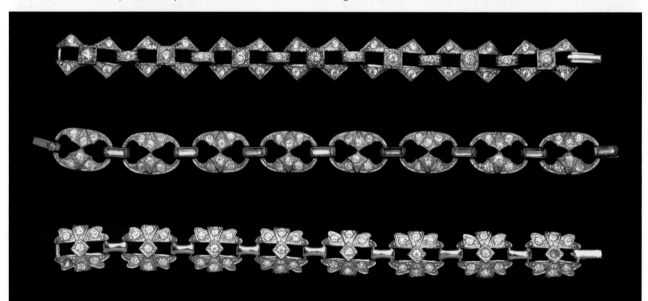

From top: Art Deco bracelet, pot metal and clear rhinestones, **$85**; Art Deco bracelet, pot metal and clear rhinestones, **$85**; bracelet, pot metal and clear rhinestones, **$95**.

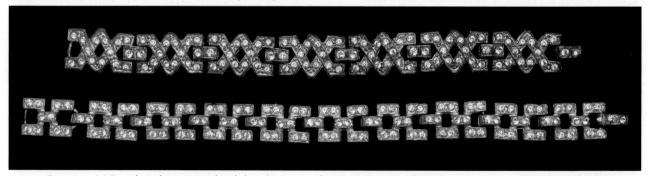

From top: Art Deco bracelet, pot metal and clear rhinestones, **$115**; Art Deco bracelet, pot metal and clear rhinestones, **$135**.

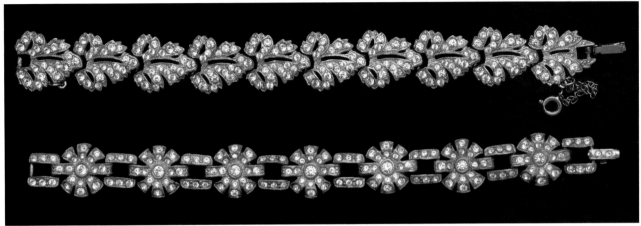

From top: leaf design bracelet, pot metal and clear rhinestones, safety chain, **$140**; flower design bracelet, pot metal and clear rhinestones, **$165**.

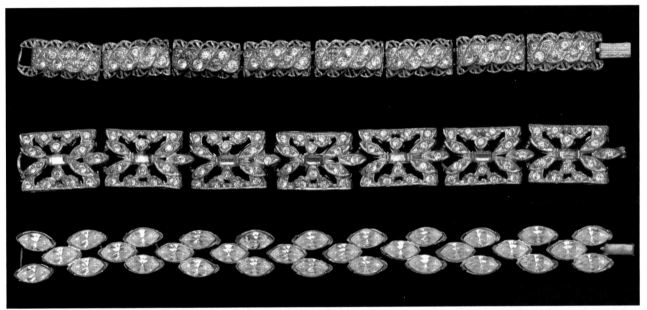

From top: bracelet, pot metal and clear rhinestones, **$88**; Art Deco bracelet, pot metal and clear rhinestones, **$145**; bracelet, pot metal and clear rhinestones, **$68**.

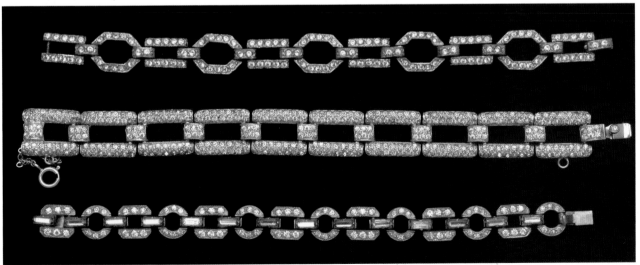

From top: Art Deco bracelet, pot metal and clear rhinestones, **$190**; Art Deco bracelet, pot metal and clear rhinestones, **$185**; Art Deco bracelet, pot metal and clear rhinestones, **$110**.

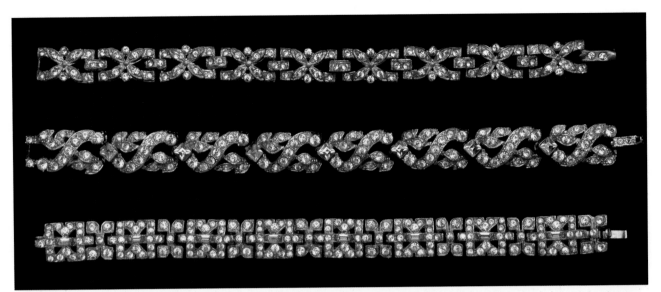

From top: floral design bracelet, pot metal and clear rhinestones, **$145**; bracelet, pot metal and clear rhinestones, **$145**; Art Deco bracelet, pot metal and clear rhinestones, **$185**.

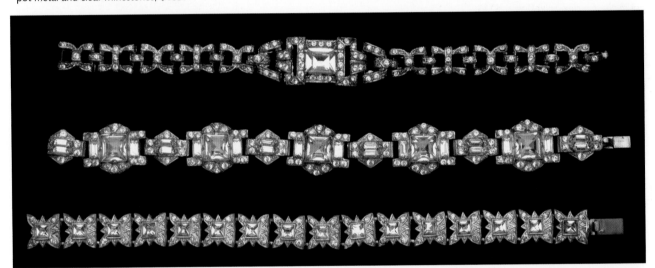

From top: Art Deco bracelet, pot metal and clear rhinestones, **$135**; Art Deco bracelet, pot metal and clear rhinestones, **$165**; Art Deco bracelet, pot metal and clear rhinestones, **$195**.

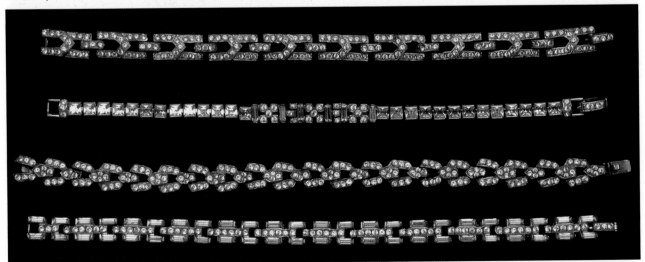

From top: Art Deco bracelet, pot metal and rhinestones, **$145**; floral design bracelet, rhodium and clear rhinestones, **$125**; Art Deco bracelet, pot metal and clear rhinestones, **$155**; Art Deco bracelet, pot metal and clear rhinestones, **$115**.

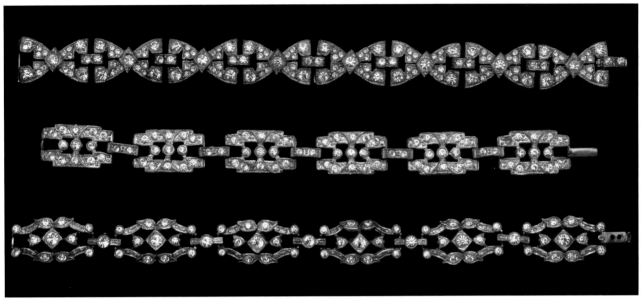

From top: Art Deco bracelet, pot metal and clear rhinestones, **$95**; Art Deco bracelet, pot metal and clear rhinestones, **$96**; Art Deco bracelet, pot metal and clear rhinestones, **$135**.

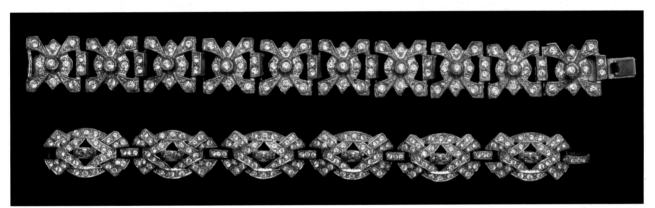

From top: Art Deco bracelet, pot metal and clear rhinestones, **$195**; Art Deco bracelet, pot metal and clear rhinestones, **$155**.

Art Deco bracelet, pot metal and clear rhinestones, **$195**.

Art Deco bracelet, rhodium and clear rhinestones, **$195**.

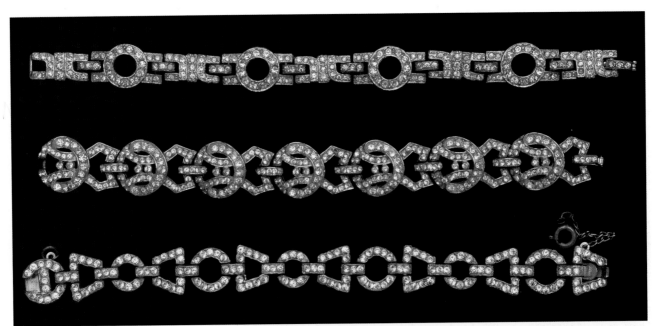

From top: Art Deco bracelet, pot metal and clear rhinestones, **$155**; Art Deco bracelet, rhodium and clear rhinestones, **$325**; Art Deco bracelet, pot metal and clear rhinestones, **$165**.

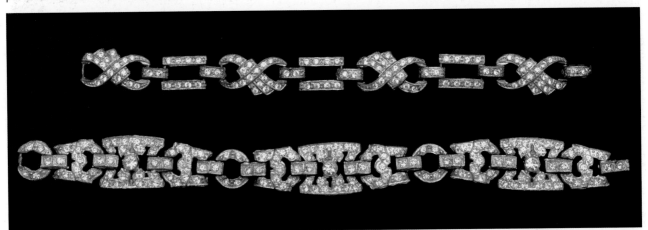

From top: Art Deco bracelet, pot metal and clear rhinestones, **$125**; Art Deco bracelet, **$135**.

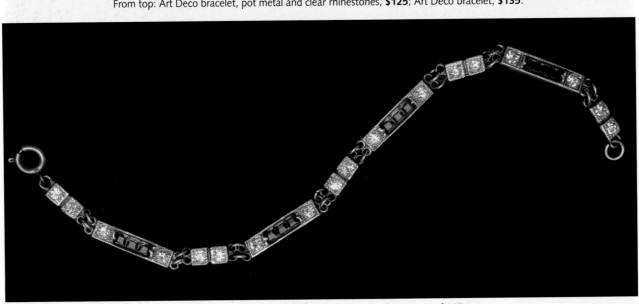

Art Deco bracelet, sterling and clear and green rhinestones, **$145**.

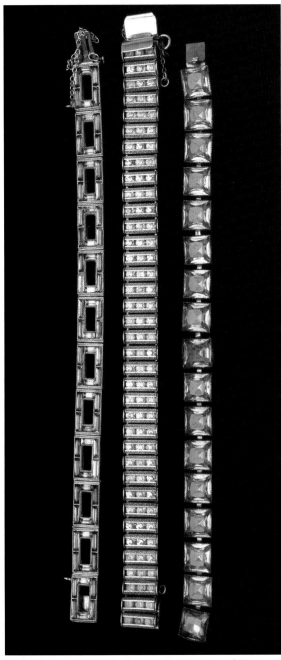

From left: bracelet, rhodium and clear rhinestones, **$110**; bracelet, sterling and clear rhinestones, **$145**; bracelet, pot metal and pink rhinestones, **$125**.

Bracelet, rhodium and clear rhinestones, clear faceted glass, **$195**.

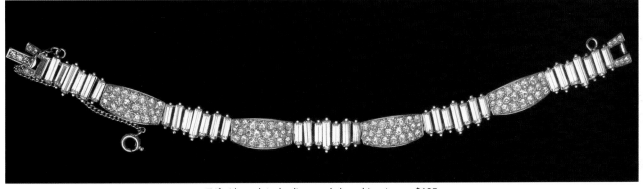

Trifari bracelet, rhodium and clear rhinestones, **$185**.

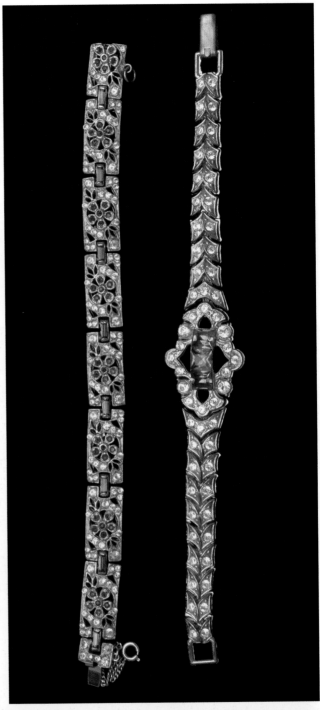

Above: TKF Art Deco bracelet, pot metal and clear and red rhinestones, blue and red glass cabochons, **$245**.
Right: flower design bracelet, rhodium and clear and blue rhinestones, **$195**; Art Deco bracelet, pot metal and clear and blue rhinestones, **$165**.

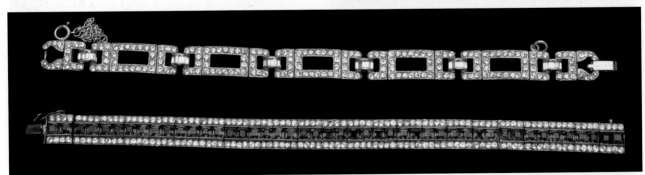

From top: B. B. Art Deco bracelet, sterling and clear rhinestones, **$285**; Art Deco bracelet, sterling and clear and green rhinestones, **$255**.

Bracelet, faux pearls with clasp made of pot metal and clear rhinestones, **$95**.

Art Deco bracelet, pot metal and clear rhinestones, glass beads, **$110**.

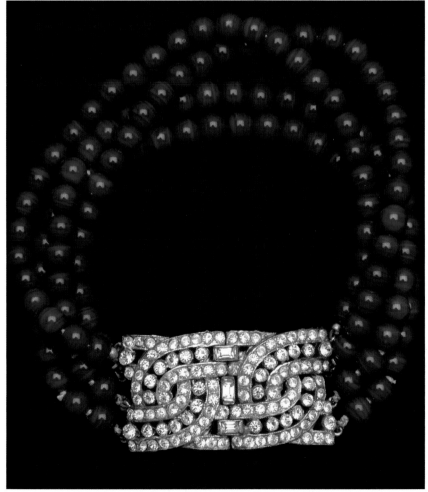

Art Deco bracelet, pot metal and clear rhinestones, blue glass beads, **$155**.

Flower bracelet, pot metal and clear rhinestones, safety chain, **$255**.

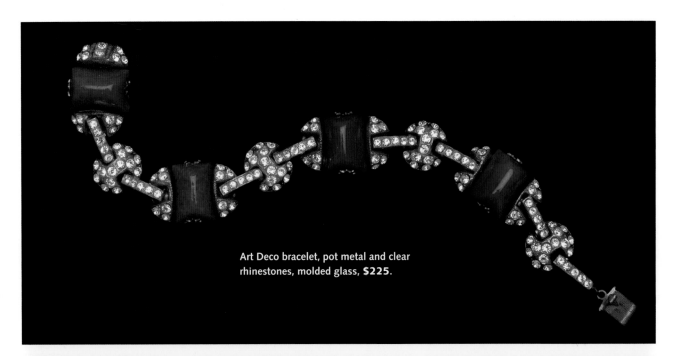

Art Deco bracelet, pot metal and clear rhinestones, molded glass, **$225**.

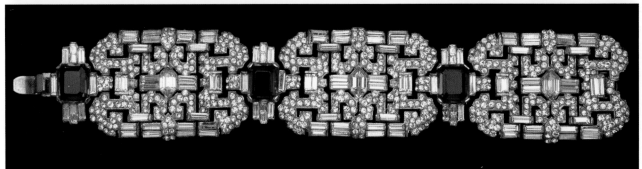

Art Deco bracelet, pot metal and clear rhinestones, faceted green glass, **$595**.

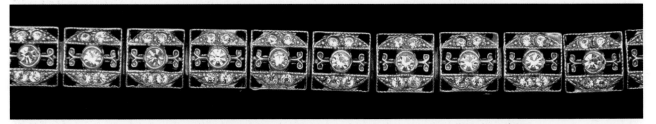

Czechoslovakian Art Deco bracelet, sterling and clear rhinestones, missing safety chain, **$295**.

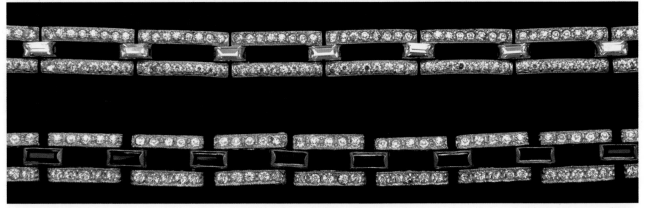

From top: Art Deco bracelet, pot metal and clear and red rhinestones, **$145**; Art Deco bracelet, pot metal and clear and black rhinestones, **$145**.

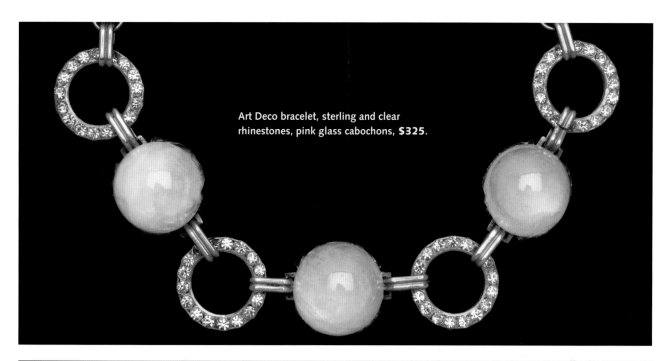

Art Deco bracelet, sterling and clear rhinestones, pink glass cabochons, **$325**.

All Co. Art Deco bow bracelet, pot metal and clear and green rhinestones, **$325**.

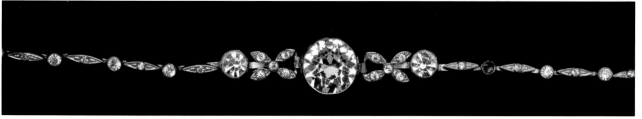

Czechoslovakian bracelet, pot metal and clear rhinestones, clear faceted glass, missing one stone, **$185**.

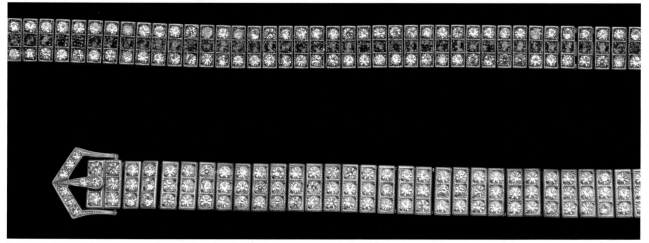

From top: Diamond Bar Art Deco bracelet, sterling and clear and red rhinestones, **$225**; Diamond Bar Art Deco buckle bracelet, sterling and clear rhinestones, **$275**.

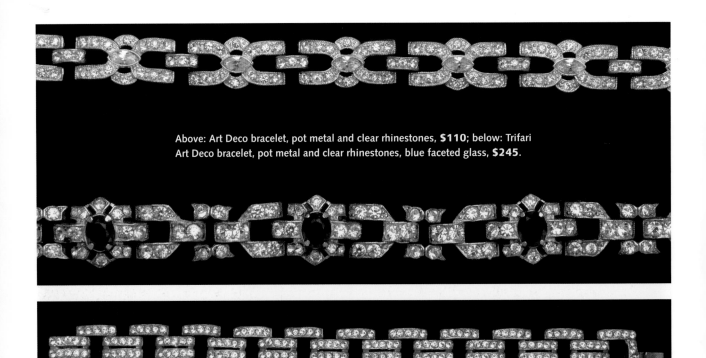

Above: Art Deco bracelet, pot metal and clear rhinestones, **$110**; below: Trifari Art Deco bracelet, pot metal and clear rhinestones, blue faceted glass, **$245**.

Art Deco bracelet, pot metal and clear rhinestones, **$285**.

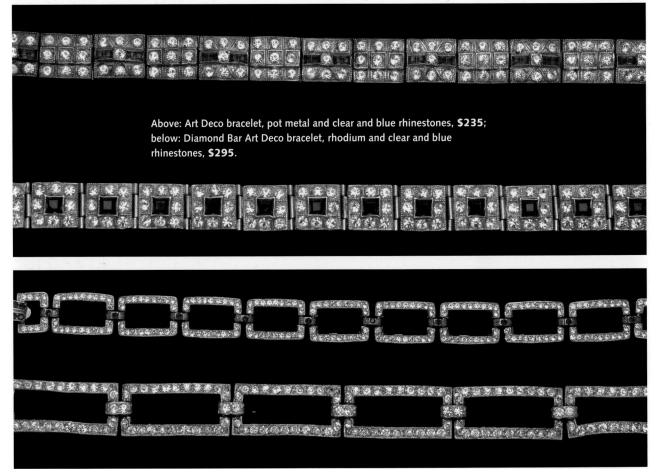

Above: Art Deco bracelet, pot metal and clear and blue rhinestones, **$235**; below: Diamond Bar Art Deco bracelet, rhodium and clear and blue rhinestones, **$295**.

From top: Art Deco bracelet, rhodium and clear and red rhinestones, **$125**; Art Deco bracelet, pot metal and clear rhinestones, **$110**.

Art Deco bracelet, pot metal and clear rhinestones, **$450**.

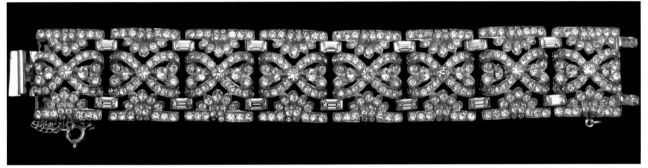

Art Deco bracelet, rhodium and clear rhinestones, **$395**.

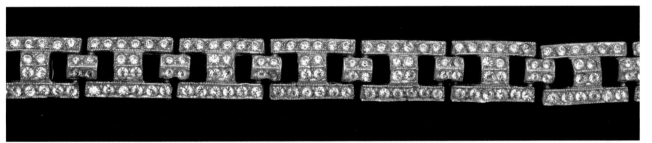

Art Deco bracelet, pot metal and clear rhinestones, safety chain, **$225**.

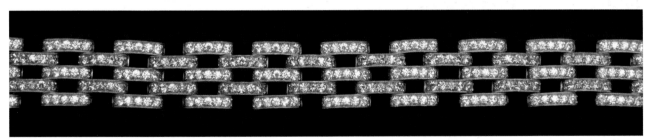

Art Deco bracelet, rhodium and clear and blue rhinestones, **$265**.

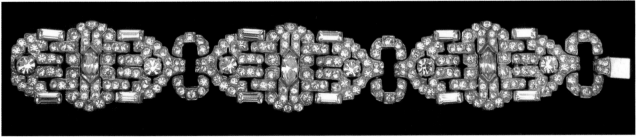

Art Deco bracelet, pot metal and clear rhinestones, **$395**.

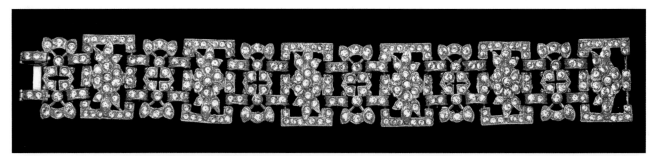

Art Deco bracelet, pot metal and clear rhinestones, **$295**.

Art Deco bracelet, sterling and clear rhinestones, green faceted glass, **$225**.

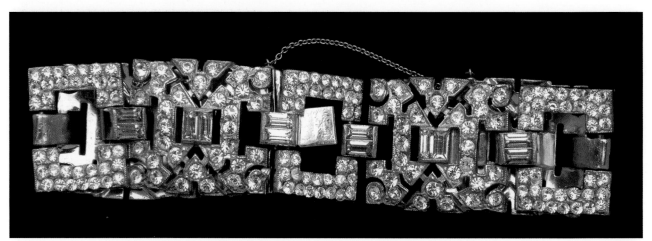

Art Deco bracelet, pot metal and clear rhinestones, **$265**.

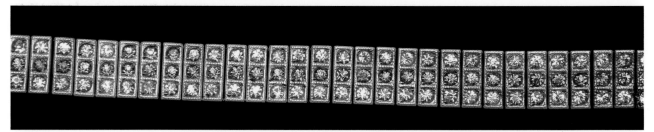

Payco Art Deco bracelet, sterling and clear and blue rhinestones, **$225**.

Bracelet, pot metal and clear rhinestones, **$165**.

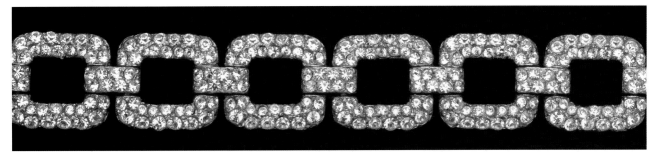

Art Deco bracelet, pot metal and clear rhinestones, **$225**.

Panetta bracelet, rhodium and clear rhinestones, **$195**.

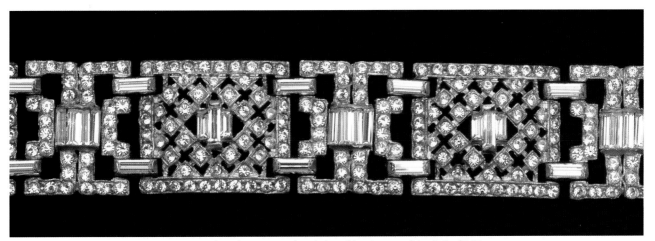

Art Deco bracelet, pot metal and clear rhinestones, safety chain, **$345**.

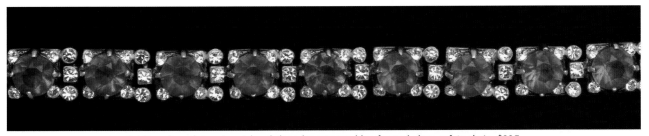

Art Deco bracelet, pot metal and clear rhinestones, blue faceted glass, safety chain, **$325**.

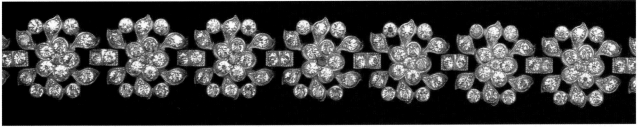

Flower bracelet, rhodium and clear rhinestones, **$195**.

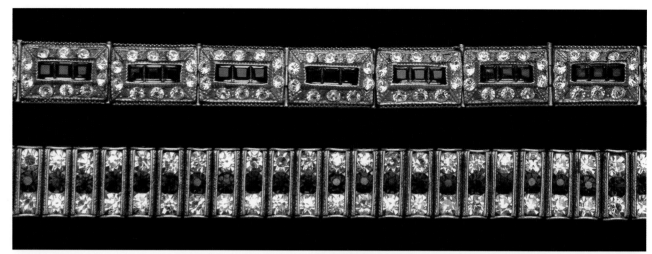

From top: Art Deco bracelet, pot metal and clear and amethyst rhinestones, **$295**; Art Deco bracelet, sterling and clear and amethyst rhinestones, **$225**.

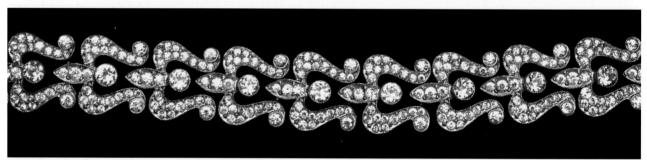

Art Deco bracelet, pot metal and clear rhinestones, **$245**.

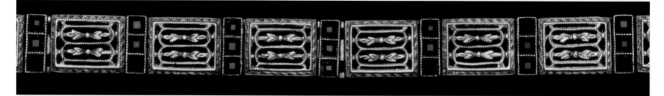

Diamond Bar Art Deco bracelet, sterling and black rhinestones, **$265**.

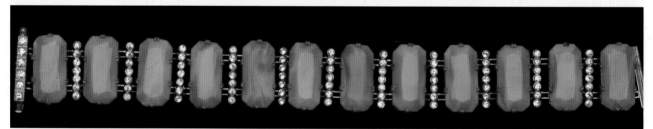

Czechoslovakian Art Deco bracelet, pot metal and clear rhinestones, green faceted glass, **$395**.

Delsa Art Deco bracelet, pot metal and clear rhinestones, blue and clear faceted glass, **$285**.

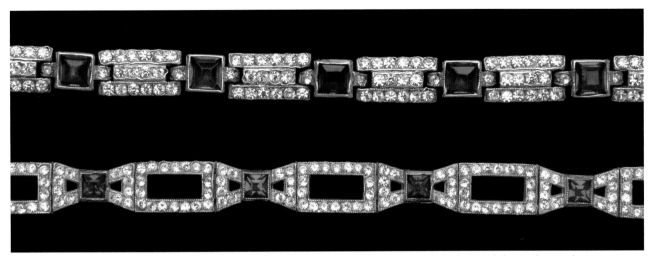

From top: Art Deco bracelet, rhodium and clear and green rhinestones, **$225;** Art Deco bracelet, rhodium and clear and green rhinestones, safety chain, **$255**.

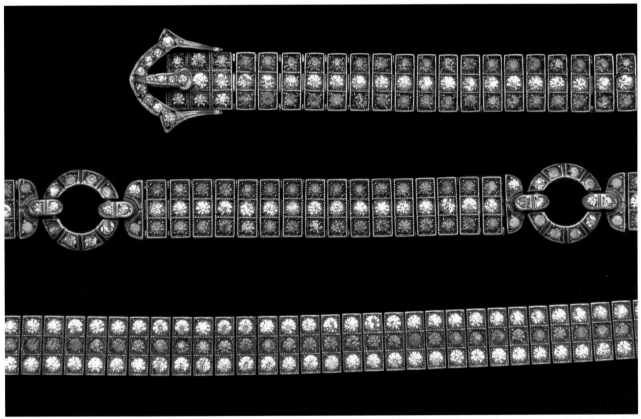

From top: Diamond Bar Art Deco buckle bracelet, sterling and clear and blue rhinestones, **$325**; Diamond Bar Art Deco bracelet, sterling and clear and blue rhinestones, **$325**; Diamond Bar Art Deco bracelet, sterling and clear and blue rhinestones, **$225**.

Art Deco bracelet, pot metal and green and clear rhinestones, **$325**.

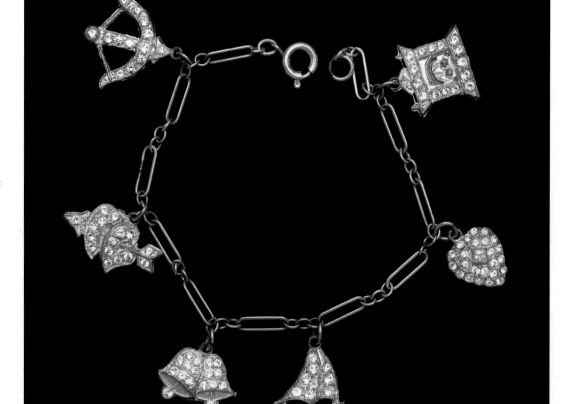

Charm bracelet, six charms, pot metal and clear and red rhinestones, **$145**.

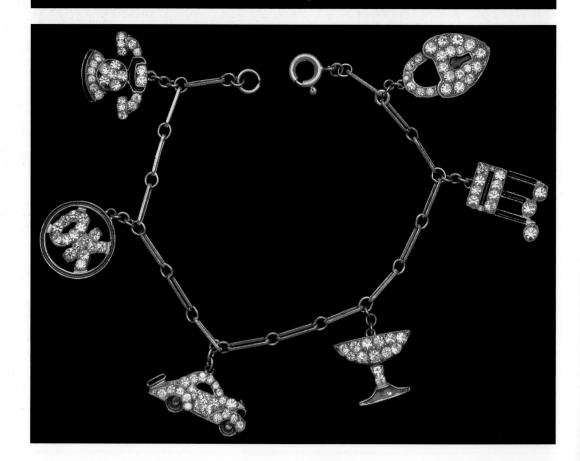

Charm bracelet, six charms, pot metal and clear rhinestones, enameling, **$145**.

Art Deco bracelet, pot metal and clear rhinestones, **$495**.

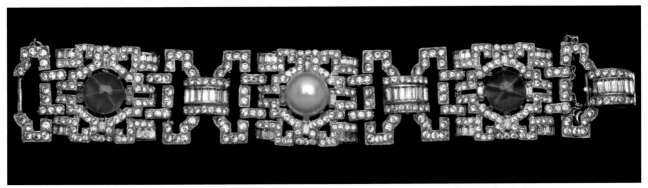

Art Deco bracelet, pot metal and clear rhinestones, blue glass cabochons, faux pearl cabochon, **$495**.

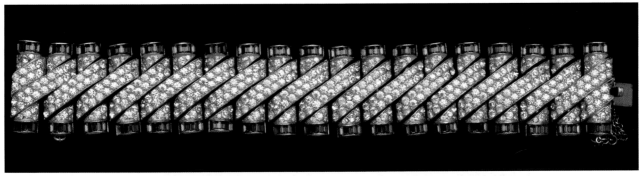

Trifari Art Deco bracelet, pot metal and clear and blue rhinestones, **$750**.

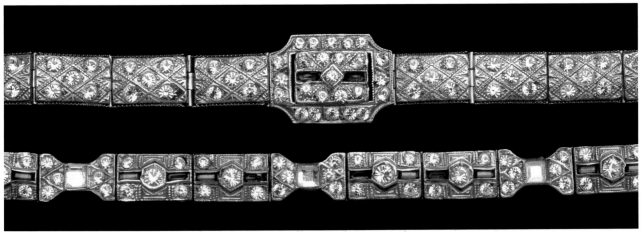

From top: Art Deco bracelet, pot metal and clear and green rhinestones, **$255**; Art Deco bracelet, rhodium and clear and green rhinestones, **$285**.

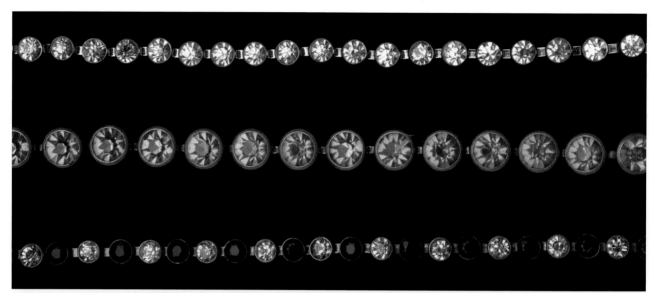

From top: Czechoslovakian bracelet, pot metal and clear rhinestones, **$95**; Czechoslovakian bracelet, pot metal and citrine rhinestones, **$125**; Czechoslovakian bracelet, pot metal and clear and black rhinestones, **$110**.

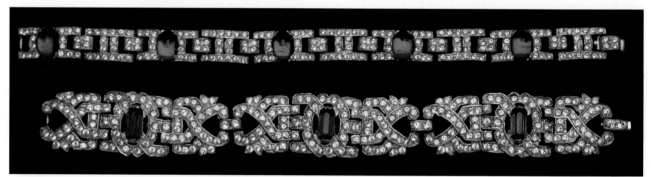

From top: Art Deco bracelet, pot metal and clear rhinestones, green glass cabochons, **$225**; Art Deco bracelet, pot metal and clear and green rhinestones, **$245**.

Left to right: TKF Art Deco bracelet with clear and blue rhinestones, **$195**; Art Deco bracelet, rhodium and clear rhinestones, pink faceted glass, **$245**; and Art Deco bracelet, rhodium and clear rhinestones, blue faceted glass, **$265**.

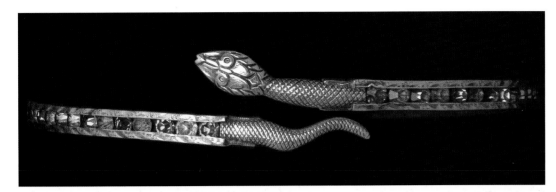

Art Deco upper arm snake bangle, sterling and green and clear rhinestones, **$285**.

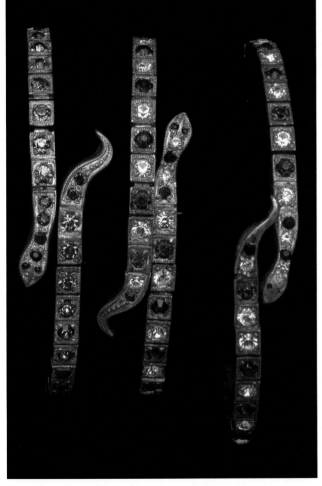

Left: Snake bangles, from left: pot metal and blue and red rhinestones, **$145**; pot metal and red and clear rhinestones, **$145**; pot metal and clear and green rhinestones, **$145**. Right: Art Deco hinged bangle, rhodium and clear rhinestones, black glass, **$145**.

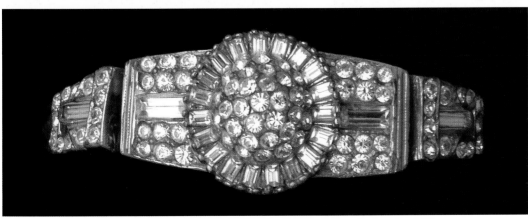

Hinged bangle, pot metal and clear rhinestones, safety chain, **$185**.

Art Deco hinged bangle, pot metal and clear and blue rhinestones, **$185**.

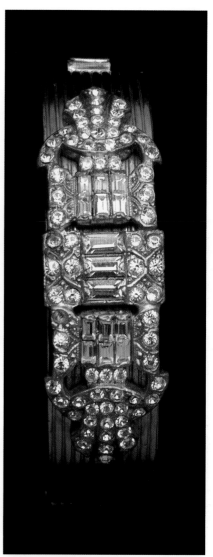

Hinged bangle, pot metal and clear rhinestones, **$185**.

Art Deco hinged bangle, pot metal and clear rhinestones, **$175**.

Art Deco snake bangle, pot metal and clear and red rhinestones, **$165**.

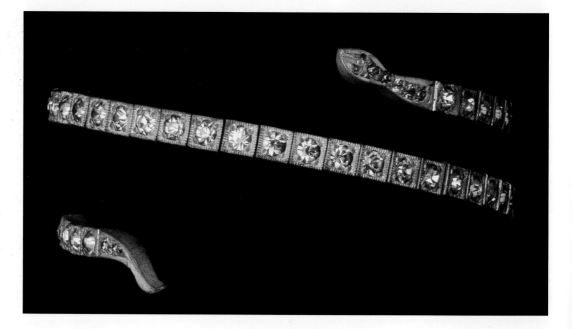

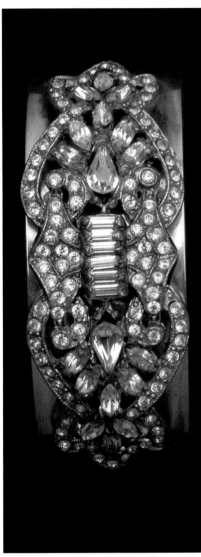

Art Deco bangle, rhodium and black rhinestones, **$145**.

Art Deco cuff, sterling and clear rhinestones, **$275**.

Art Deco hinged bangle, rhodium and clear rhinestones, safety chain, **$295**.

Art Deco hinged bangle, pot metal and clear and blue rhinestones, **$125**.

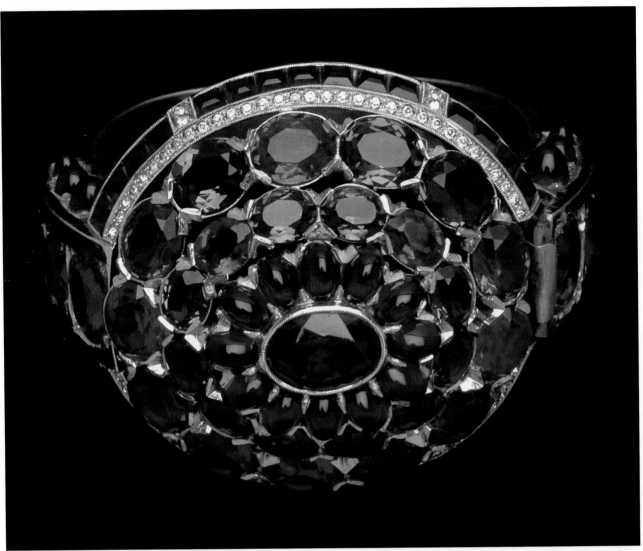

Art Deco hinged bangle, pot metal and clear and green rhinestones, faceted green, fuchsia, blue, and citrine faceted glass, red and green glass cabochons, **$975**.

Art Deco hinged bangle, pot metal and clear and green rhinestones, **$135**.

Bangle, pot metal and blue rhinestones, **$65**.

Art Deco hinged bangle, pot metal and clear rhinestones, **$145**.

Art Deco hinged bangle, pot metal and clear and green rhinestones, **$155**.

Fishson Art Deco bangle, silverite and clear and amethyst rhinestones, **$185**.

Buckle cuff, pot metal and green and clear rhinestones, **$450**.

Hinged bangle, pot metal and clear rhinestones, safety chain, **$145**.

From left: Art Deco double row hinged bangle, pot metal and clear and green rhinestones, **$265**; Art Deco double row hinged bangle, sterling and clear rhinestones, **$295**.

Floral hinged bangle, pot metal and clear rhinestones, **$225**.

Brooches
& Pins

Pierce floral watch pin, rhodium and clear rhinestones, faux pearl, enameling, wear to enamel, **$495**.

Brooch, pot metal and clear rhinestones, faux pearls, **$145**.

Reja brooch, sterling and clear and green rhinestones and faux pearls, **$195**.

Bird brooch, pot metal and clear and blue rhinestones, **$155**.

Art Deco brooch, pot metal and clear rhinestones, **$195**.

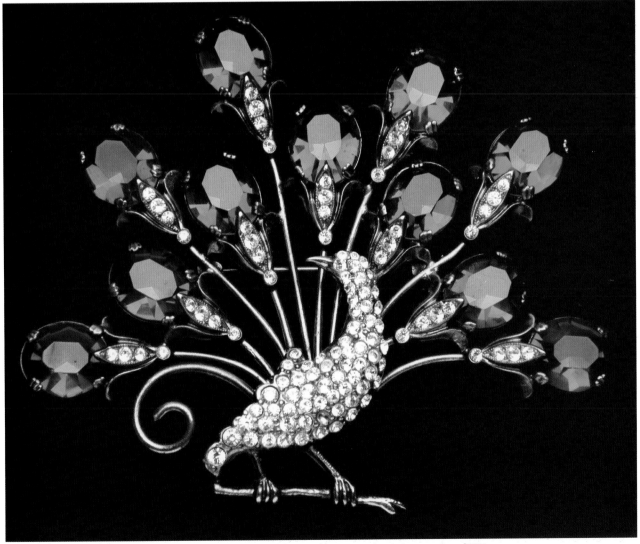

Peacock brooch, sterling and green rhinestones, faceted green glass, **$285**.

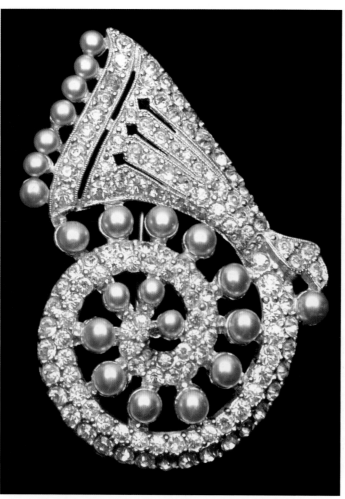

Brooch, pot metal and clear rhinestones, faux pearls, **$125**.

Leaf design brooch, pot metal and clear rhinestones, **$165**.

Flower brooch, pot metal, celluloid flower, clear rhinestones, blue paint, **$165**.

Floral design brooch, pot metal and clear rhinestones and blue cabochons, **$190**.

Art Deco brooch, pot metal and clear and green rhinestones, **$185**.

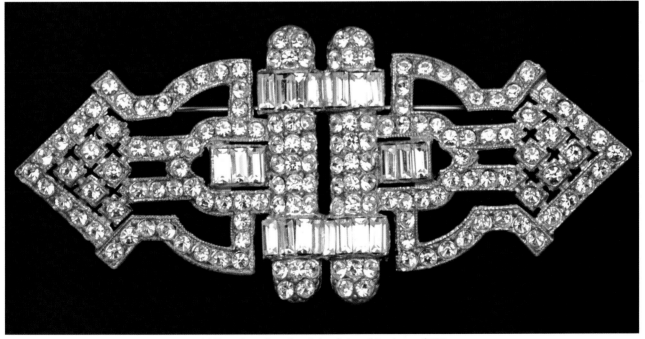

Art Deco brooch, pot metal and clear rhinestones, **$185**.

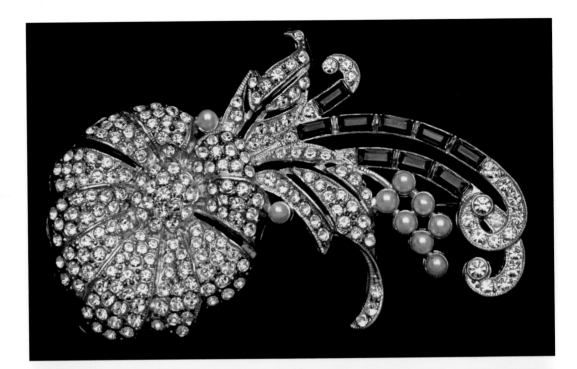

Floral brooch, pot metal, clear and green rhinestones, faux pearls, **$195**.

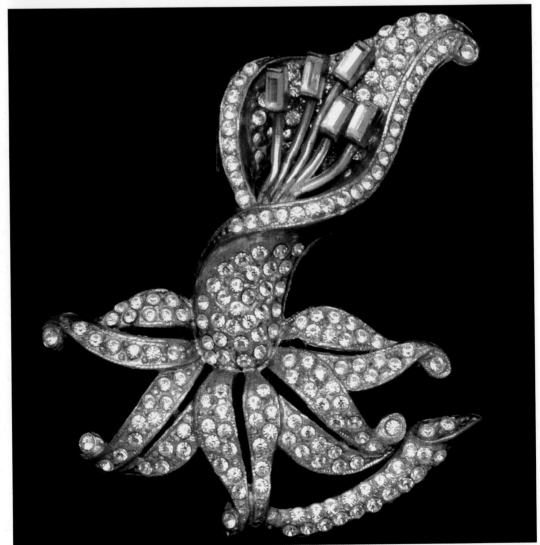

Flower brooch, pot metal and clear rhinestones, **$195**.

Corocraft bird brooch, rhodium and clear rhinestones, **$110**.

Snowflake brooch, rhodium and clear rhinestones, clear faceted glass, **$95**.

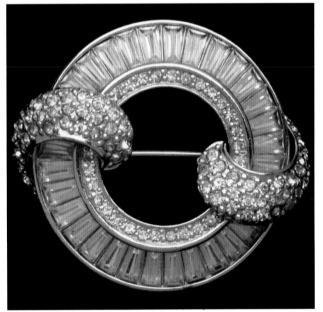

Pennino brooch, rhodium and clear rhinestones, **$125**.

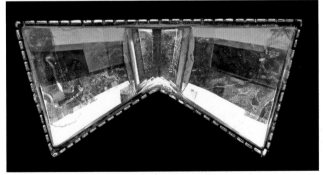

Bow brooch, pot metal and foil back glass, **$55**.

Bow brooch, pot metal and clear rhinestones, **$98**.

Art Deco brooch, pot metal and clear rhinestones, **$165**.

Art Deco brooch, pot metal and clear rhinestones, **$135**.

Bogoff flower
brooch, pot
metal and clear
rhinestones, **$165**.

Bow brooch, pot
metal and clear and
blue rhinestones,
$188.

Flower urn brooch, pot metal and red, green, blue, citrine, peridot, and pink rhinestones, **$95**.

Butterfly brooch, pot metal and clear rhinestones, **$195**.

Art Deco brooch,
pot metal and clear
and red rhinestones,
red glass cabochon,
$135.

Leaf brooch,
rhodium and clear
rhinestones, **$110**.

Bow brooch, rhodium and clear rhinestones, **$88**.

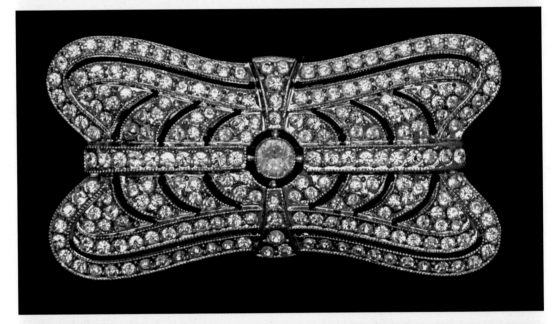

Art Deco brooch, rhodium and clear rhinestones, **$185**.

TKF Art Deco brooch, rhodium and clear rhinestones, **$295**.

Art Deco bow brooch, rhodium and clear rhinestones, green faceted glass, **$185**.

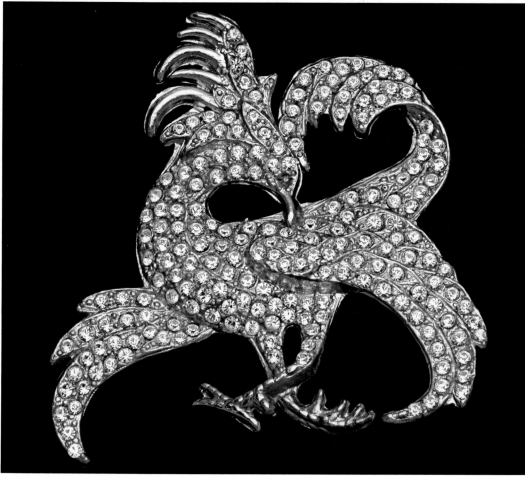

Bird brooch, pot metal and clear and green rhinestones, **$195**.

Bow brooch, pot metal and clear rhinestones, **$188**.

Floral brooch, pot metal and clear rhinestones, citrine faceted glass, **$185**.

Bow brooch, pot metal and clear rhinestones, opalescent plastic cabochons, **$110**.

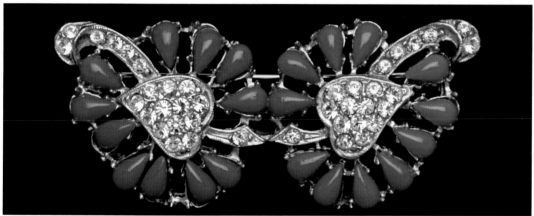

Art Deco leaf brooch, pot metal and clear rhinestones, coral-colored glass cabochons, **$95**.

Butterfly brooch, pot metal and clear, blue and red rhinestones, **$110**.

Retro brooch, rhodium and clear and green rhinestones, **$135**.

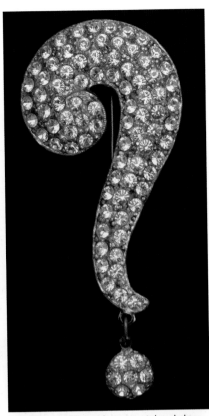

Flower basket brooch, rhodium and clear rhinestones, molded glass flowers and leaves, **$225**.

Question mark brooch, pot metal and clear rhinestones, **$95**.

Flower basket brooch, pot metal and clear, pink, light blue, citrine, and peridot rhinestones, **$145**.

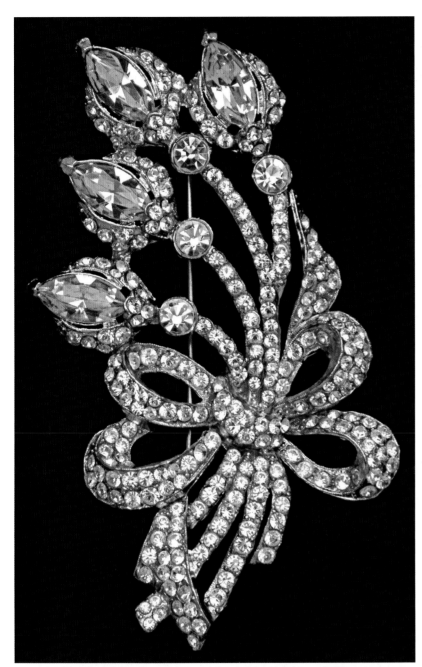

Floral design brooch, pot metal and clear rhinestones, **$185**.

Art Deco brooch, pot metal and clear rhinestones, **$120**.

Flower brooch, pot metal and clear and red rhinestones, **$98**.

From top: Art Deco bow brooch, pot metal and clear rhinestones, **$185**; Art Deco bow brooch, pot metal and clear rhinestones, **$65**.

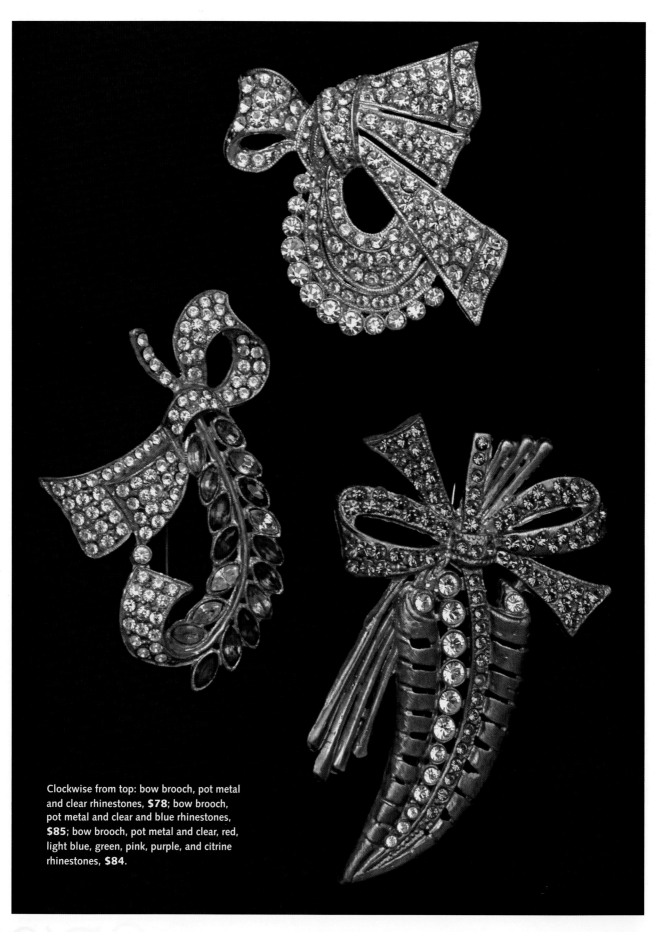

Clockwise from top: bow brooch, pot metal and clear rhinestones, **$78**; bow brooch, pot metal and clear and blue rhinestones, **$85**; bow brooch, pot metal and clear, red, light blue, green, pink, purple, and citrine rhinestones, **$84**.

Moon brooch, rhodium and clear rhinestones, a few dark stones, **$95**.

Reja brooch, rhodium and clear rhinestones, clear faceted glass, **$165**.

Retro brooch, rhodium and clear rhinestones, **$125**.

Art Deco brooch, pot metal and clear rhinestones, red glass cabochons, **$115**.

Trifari leaf brooch, pot metal and clear rhinestones, **$225**.

Floral brooch, pot metal and clear rhinestones, faux pearls, enameling, **$185**.

Art Deco brooch, rhodium and clear rhinestones, **$210**.

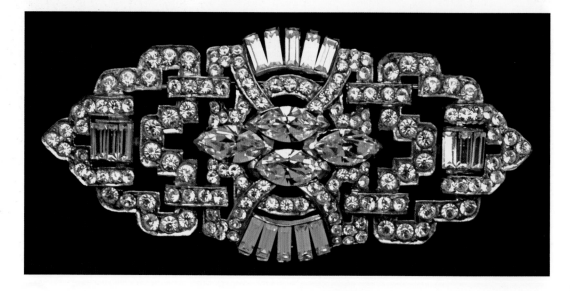

Joseph Wiesner leaf brooch, rhodium and clear and blue rhinestones, **$130**.

Trifari Art Deco brooch, sterling and clear rhinestones, **$245**.

Brooch, pot metal and clear rhinestones, **$78**.

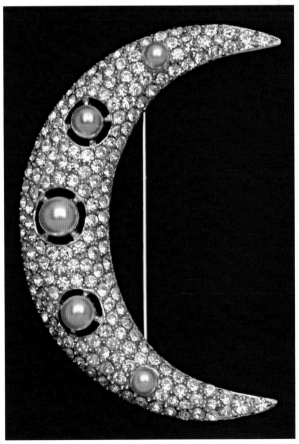

Moon brooch, rhodium and clear rhinestones, faux pearls, **$110**.

Flower brooch, rhodium and clear rhinestones, blue faceted glass, **$225**.

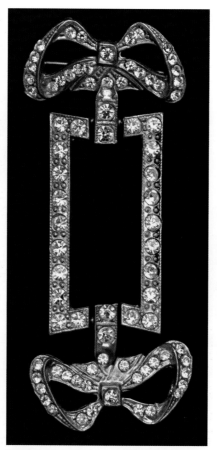

Bow brooch, pot metal and clear rhinestones, **$125**.

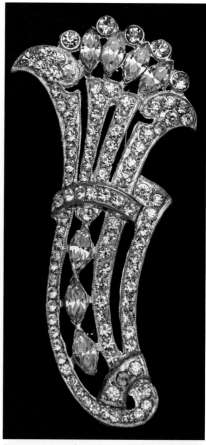

Staret Art Deco brooch, pot metal and clear rhinestones, **$185**.

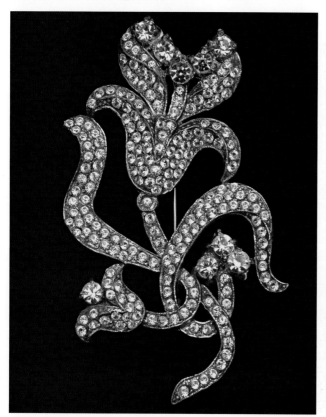

Floral brooch, pot metal and clear rhinestones, **$165**.

Flower brooch, rhodium and clear rhinestones, **$135**.

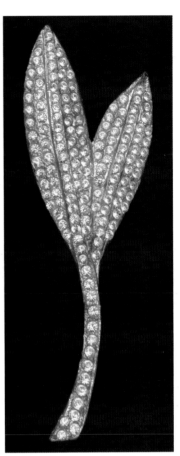

Eisenberg Original leaf brooch, pot metal and clear rhinestones, **$285**.

Lantern brooch, lantern moves, rhodium and clear and green rhinestones, **$125**.

Leaf brooch, pot metal and clear rhinestones, **$85**.

Kramer leaf brooch, rhodium and clear rhinestones, **$110**.

Mazer floral brooch, rhodium and clear rhinestones, enameling, **$245**.

Cockatoo brooch, pot metal and clear rhinestones, enameling, **$85**.

Floral bouquet brooch, pot metal and clear, red, green, and citrine rhinestones, enameling, some wear to enamel, **$45**.

Lily brooch, pot metal and clear rhinestones, enameling, **$128**.

Floral brooch, pot metal with a gold wash, clear rhinestones, faux pearls, and enameling, **$165**.

Flower brooch, pot metal with gold wash, blue rhinestones and enameling, **$65**.

Lily brooch, pot metal with gold wash, clear rhinestones, orange glass beads, enameling, **$125**.

From left: flower brooch, trembler, pot metal and clear and purple rhinestones, enameling, **$145**; floral brooch, pot metal and clear rhinestones, enameling, **$110**.

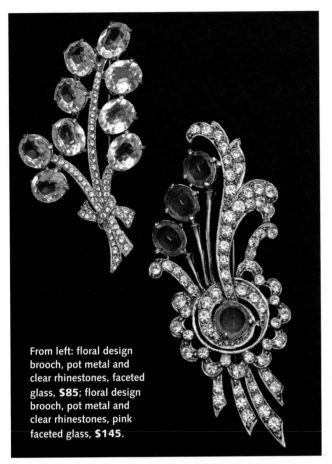

From left: floral design brooch, pot metal and clear rhinestones, faceted glass, **$85**; floral design brooch, pot metal and clear rhinestones, pink faceted glass, **$145**.

Flower brooch, pot metal and clear rhinestones, red, green, and blue faceted glass, enameling, **$110**.

From top: floral brooch, pot metal and clear rhinestones, faux pearl and enameling, some wear to enameling, **$72**; floral brooch, pot metal and green rhinestones, enameling, some wear to enameling, **$98**.

From top: flower brooch, pot metal and clear rhinestones, faux pearls, **$95**; flower brooch, pot metal and clear rhinestones, **$42**.

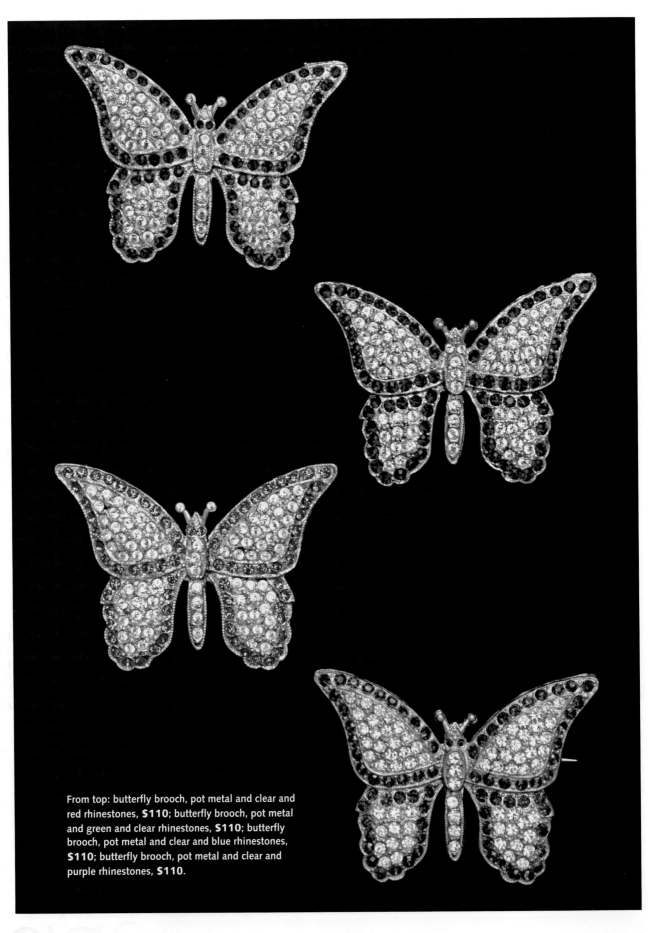

From top: butterfly brooch, pot metal and clear and red rhinestones, **$110**; butterfly brooch, pot metal and green and clear rhinestones, **$110**; butterfly brooch, pot metal and clear and blue rhinestones, **$110**; butterfly brooch, pot metal and clear and purple rhinestones, **$110**.

From left: flower brooch, pot metal and clear rhinestones, enameling, **$145**; flower brooch, pot metal and clear rhinestones, enameling, some wear to enamel, **$125**; double flower brooch, pot metal and clear rhinestones, enameling, some wear to the enamel, **$120**.

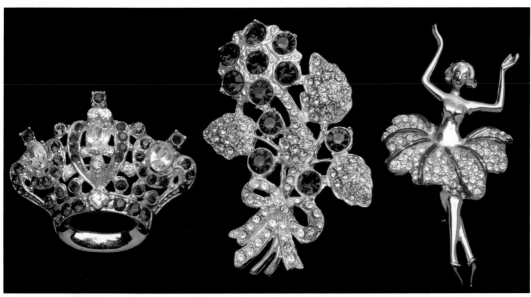

From left: Coro crown brooch, pot metal and clear, red, green, purple, and citrine rhinestones, **$92**; flower brooch, pot metal and clear, green, and purple rhinestones, **$36**; ballerina brooch, rhodium and clear rhinestones, enameling, **$95**.

From left: Shoemaker & Pickering Co. lily brooch, trembler, pot metal and clear rhinestones, lavender and pink enameling, **$125**; lily trembler brooch, pot metal with a gold wash, pink and white enameling, clear rhinestones, **$168**.

From left: bow brooch, pot metal and clear rhinestones, **$85**; bow brooch, pot metal and clear rhinestones, **$110**.

Below from left: floral brooch, pot metal and blue rhinestones, **$68**; floral bouquet brooch, pot metal and clear and blue rhinestones, **$95**.

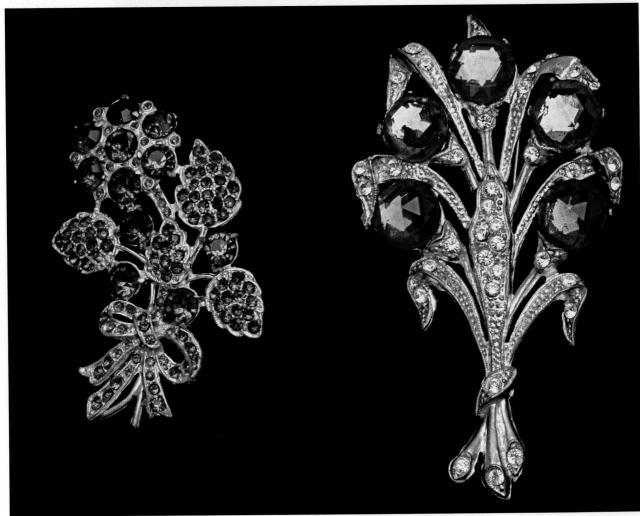

Above from left: Trifari brooch, rhodium and clear rhinestones, clear faceted glass, **$165**; flower design brooch, rhodium and clear and green rhinestones, **$165**.

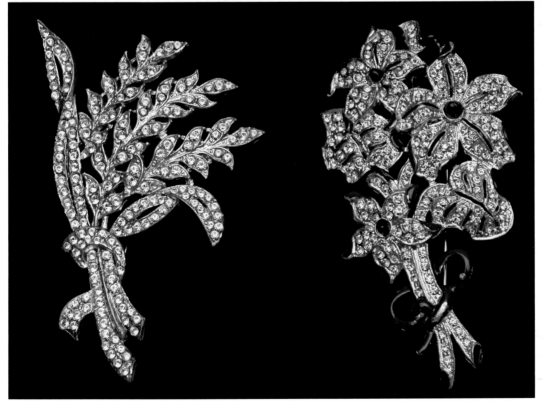

From left: bouquet brooch, pot metal and clear rhinestones, **$150**; floral bouquet brooch, pot metal and clear rhinestones, purple glass cabochons, enameling, some wear to enamel, **$110**.

From left: Trifari floral brooch, sterling and clear rhinestones, clear faceted glass, **$195**; Trifari floral brooch, pot metal and clear rhinestones, **$155**.

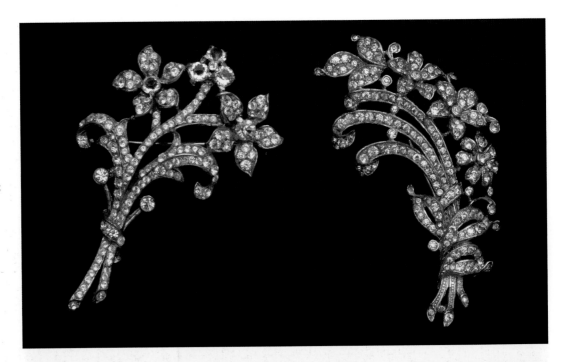

From left: bow brooch, pot metal and clear and red rhinestones, **$145**; bow brooch, pot metal and clear and blue rhinestones, **$155**.

From left: flower brooch, pot metal and clear rhinestones, **$48**; flower brooch, pot metal and clear rhinestones, **$55**; flower brooch, pot metal and clear rhinestones, **$75**.

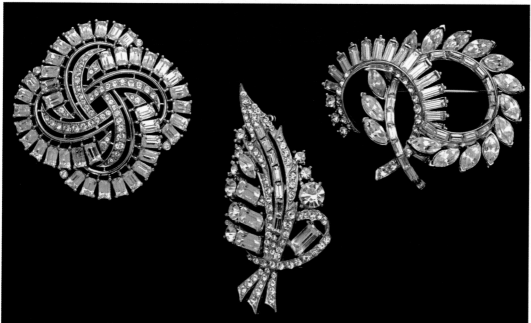

Above from left: bird brooch, pot metal and clear and blue rhinestones, **$135**; bird brooch, pot metal and clear and red rhinestones, **$135**.

From left: Trifari retro brooch, rhodium and clear rhinestones, **$125**; leaf brooch, pot metal and clear rhinestones, **$85**; Corocraft retro brooch, rhodium and clear rhinestones, **$110**.

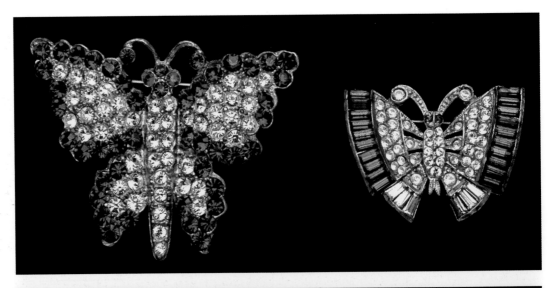

From left: butterfly brooch, pot metal and clear, green, and red rhinestones, **$95**; Art Deco butterfly, pot metal and clear and green rhinestones, **$135**.

From left: flower brooch, pot metal with gold wash, pink faceted glass, enameling, black rhinestone, **$85**; flower brooch, pot metal and clear rhinestones, blue faceted glass, enameling, **$125**.

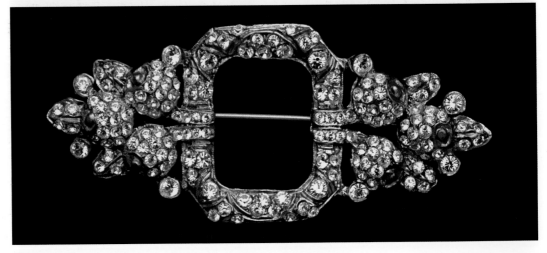

Art Deco brooch, pot metal and clear rhinestones, **$175**.

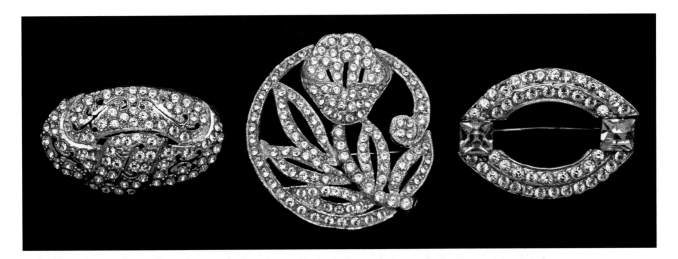

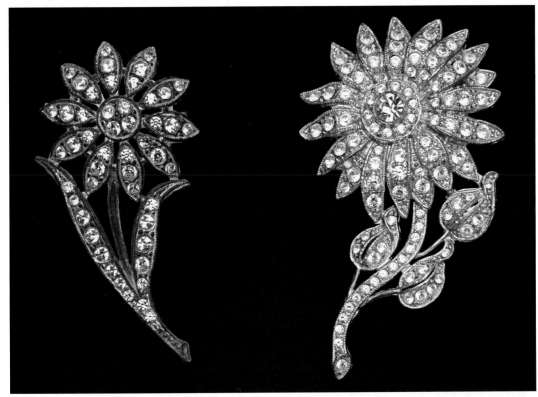

Above from left:
Art Deco brooch,
pot metal and clear
rhinestones, **$98**;
floral brooch, pot
metal and clear
rhinestones, **$140**;
Art Deco brooch,
pot metal and clear
rhinestones, **$85**.

From left: flower
brooch, pot
metal and clear
rhinestones, **$55**;
flower brooch, pot
metal and clear
rhinestones, **$155**.

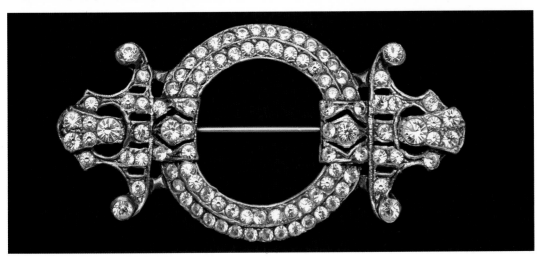

Art Deco brooch,
pot metal and clear
rhinestones, **$145**.

From left: Art Deco brooch, pot metal and clear and red rhinestones, **$98**; arrow brooch, pot metal and clear and blue rhinestones, **$65**; leaf design brooch, pot metal and clear rhinestones, **$68**.

From left: Art Deco brooch, pot metal and clear and purple rhinestones, **$185**; Art Deco brooch, pot metal and clear rhinestones, **$98**.

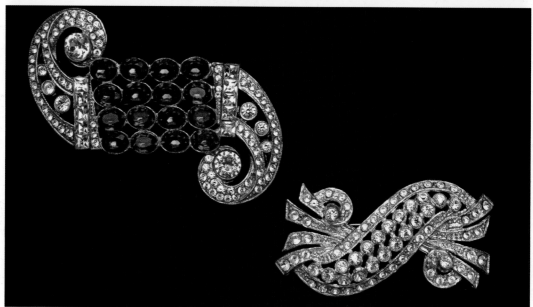

From left: Gems Co. brooch, pot metal and clear and red rhinestones, **$55**; musical clef brooch, pot metal and clear rhinestones, **$58**; heart brooch, pot metal and clear and red rhinestones, **$95**.

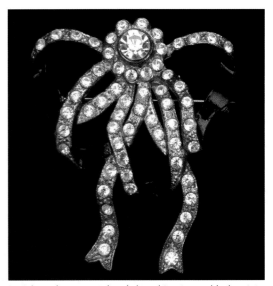

Bow brooch, pot metal and clear rhinestones, black paint, **$62**.

From top: Art Deco brooch, pot metal and clear rhinestones, **$110**; Art Deco brooch, pot metal and clear rhinestones, **$110**; Art Deco brooch, pot metal and clear rhinestones, **$125**.

Bow brooch, pot metal and clear rhinestones, black enameling, **$98**.

From left: Eiffel Tower brooch, rhodium and clear rhinestones, **$65**; horse brooch, pot metal and clear rhinestones, **$48**; Ora cross brooch, pot metal and clear rhinestones, **$34**.

Bird brooch, pot metal and clear rhinestones, enameling, **$195**.

From left: bird brooch, pot metal and clear and blue rhinestones, blue plastic cabochons, enameling, **$98**; bird brooch, rhodium and clear and blue rhinestones, **$160**; eagle brooch, pot metal and clear and red rhinestones, **$88**.

Above: Marcel Boucher bird brooch, rhodium and clear rhinestones, faux pearls, enameling, **$325.**

From left: bird brooch, pot metal with gold wash and clear rhinestones, enameling, some wear to enamel, **$65**; double cockatoo brooch, pot metal and clear and blue rhinestones, enameling, **$88**; bird brooch, pot metal and clear rhinestones, purple faceted glass, enameling, **$110.**

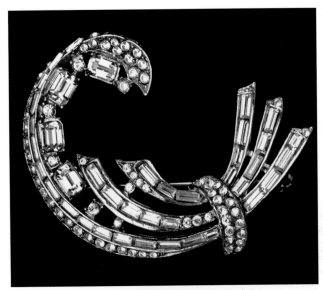

Brooch, rhodium and clear rhinestones, **$125.**

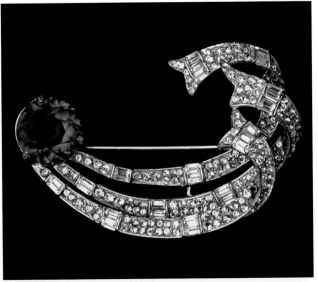

Halbe brooch, rhodium and clear and green rhinestones, **$165.**

From left: leaf brooch, pot metal and clear rhinestones, faux pearls, **$48**; Art Deco brooch, pot metal and clear rhinestones, faux pearls, **$65**.

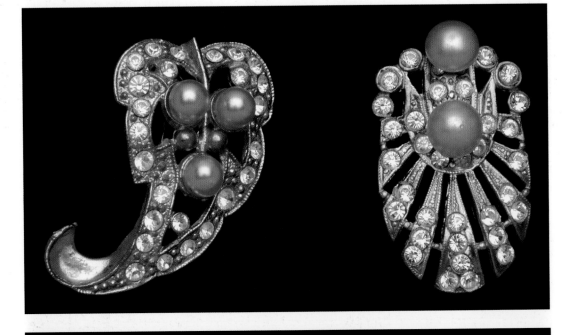

From left: Art Deco brooch, rhodium and clear and green rhinestones, **$60**; brooch, pot metal and clear rhinestones, **$85**.

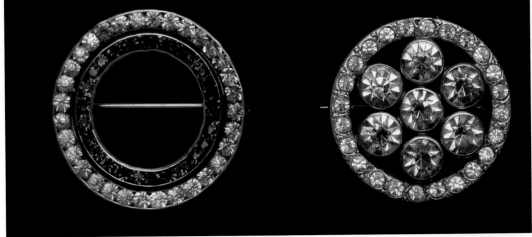

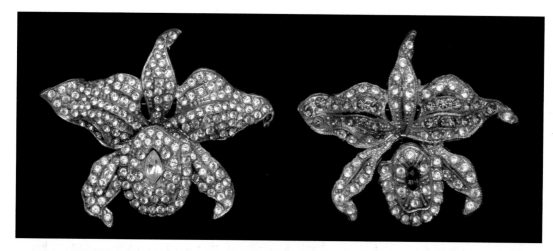

From left: lily trembler brooch, pot metal and clear rhinestones, **$155**; lily trembler brooch, pot metal and clear and blue rhinestones, **$155**.

From left: basket brooch, pot metal and clear rhinestones, pink plastic cabochons, **$95**; basket brooch, pot metal and clear rhinestones, green flat back rhinestones, **$80**.

From left: floral bouquet brooch, pot metal and clear and blue rhinestones, **$165**; Coro floral bouquet brooch, pot metal and clear rhinestones, **$145**.

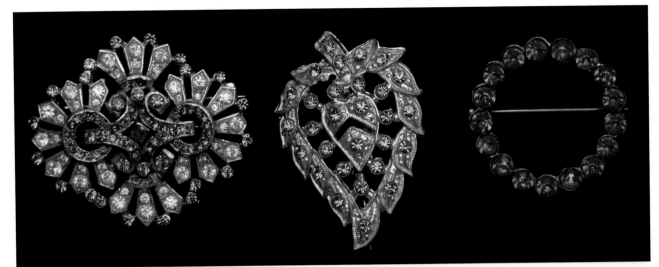

From left: Art Deco brooch, pot metal and clear and blue rhinestones, **$88**; leaf brooch, pot metal and blue rhinestones, **$28**; circle pin, pot metal and clear rhinestones, **$12**.

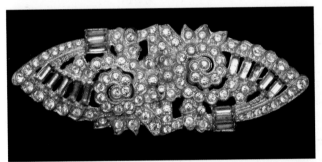

Art Deco floral design brooch, pot metal and clear rhinestones, **$90**.

Art Deco brooch, pot metal and clear rhinestones, red cabochons, **$88**.

Bow brooch, rhodium and clear rhinestones, enameling, **$245**.

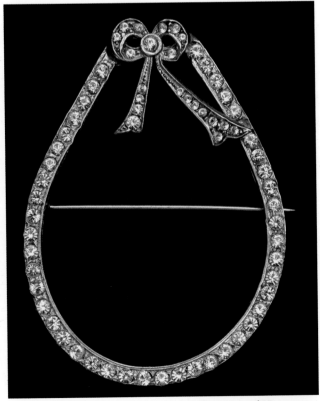

Bow brooch, pot metal and clear rhinestones, **$85**.

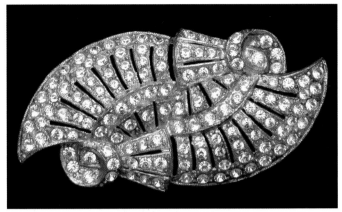

Art Deco brooch, pot metal and clear rhinestones, **$145**.

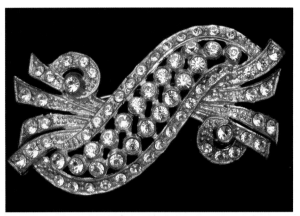

Art Deco brooch, pot metal and clear rhinestones, **$98**.

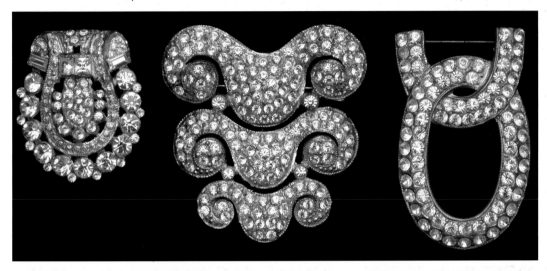

From left: Art Deco brooch, pot metal and clear rhinestones, **$68**; Art Deco brooch, pot metal and clear rhinestones, **$165**, Art Deco brooch, pot metal and clear rhinestones, **$92**.

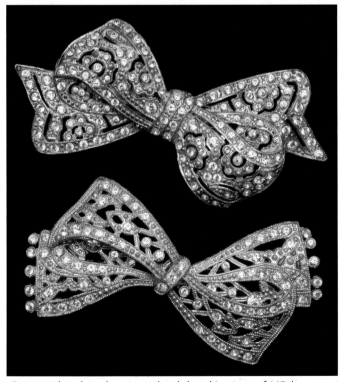

From top: bow brooch, pot metal and clear rhinestones, **$145**; bow brooch, pot metal and clear rhinestones, **$95**.

From top: Art Deco bow brooch, rhodium and clear rhinestones, **$110**; bow brooch, pot metal and clear rhinestones, **$68**.

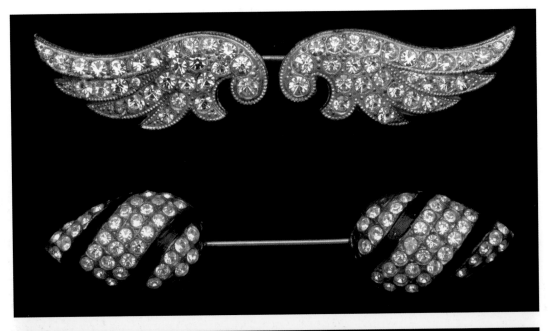

From top: Art Deco brooch, pot metal and clear rhinestones, one wing twists off to open and close the pin, **$88**; Art Deco brooch, pot metal and clear rhinestones, enameling, one side twists off to open and close the pin, **$62**.

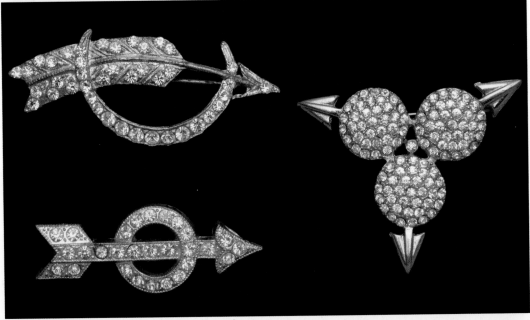

Clockwise from top left: bow and arrow brooch, pot metal and clear rhinestones, **$68**; Art Deco brooch, pot metal and clear rhinestones, **$88**; arrow brooch, pot metal and clear rhinestones, **$32**.

From left: bow brooch, rhodium and clear rhinestones, **$85**; bow brooch, pot metal and clear rhinestones, **$48**; Art Deco bow brooch, pot metal and clear rhinestones, **$42**.

Art Deco brooch,
pot metal and clear
rhinestones, clear
faceted glass, **$325**.

Brooch, pot metal
and rhinestones,
$185.

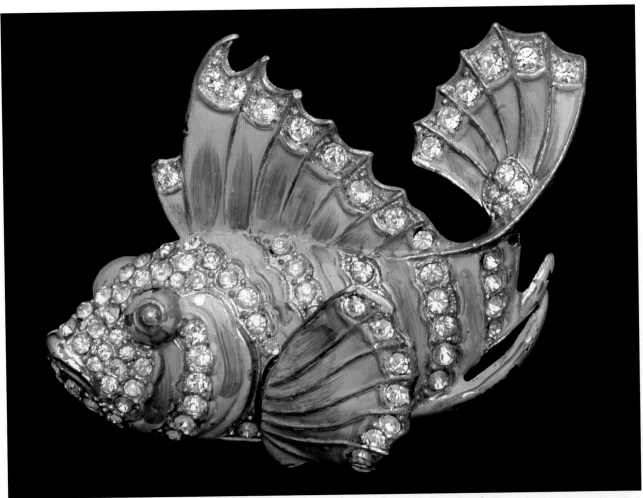

Three-dimensional fish brooch, pot metal and clear rhinestones, enameling, **$265**.

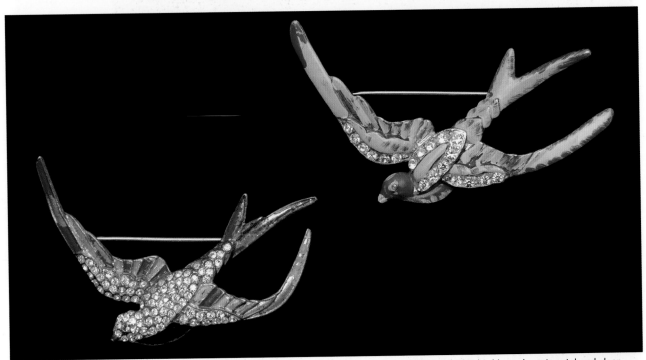

From left: bird brooch, pot metal and clear and blue rhinestones, enameling, some wear to enamel, **$110**; bird brooch, pot metal and clear rhinestones, enameling, **$95**.

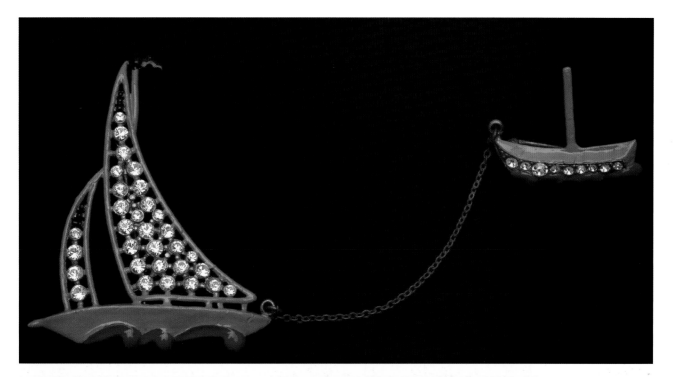

Above: double boat brooch, pot metal and clear rhinestones, enameling, **$125**.

Sailfish brooch, pot metal and clear and green rhinestones, enameling, **$145**.

Flower brooch, pot metal and clear rhinestones, blue faceted glass, **$125**.

Art Deco brooch, pot metal and clear rhinestones, clear faceted glass, **$195**.

Flower brooch, pot metal and clear and blue rhinestones, **$110**.

Art Deco brooch, pot metal and clear, green, and topaz rhinestones, **$135**.

Doctor Dress brooch, pot metal and clear rhinestones, **$165**.

Reinad star brooch, rhodium and clear rhinestones, **$225**.

Floral bouquet brooch, pot metal and clear rhinestones, clear faceted glass, **$165**.

Art Deco brooch, pot metal and clear rhinestones, clear faceted glass, **$245**.

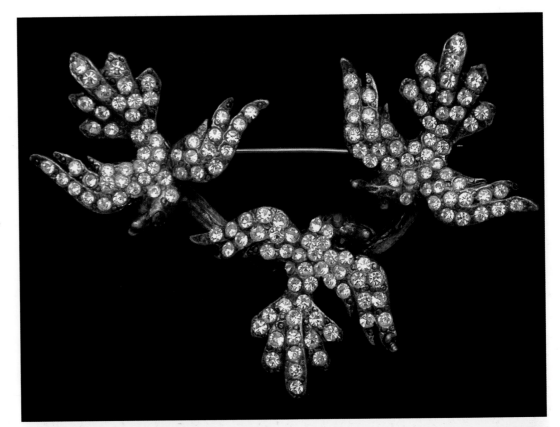

Three-bird brooch,
pot metal and clear
and red rhinestones,
$145.

Peacock brooch,
pot metal and clear
rhinestones, red
faceted glass, **$210**.

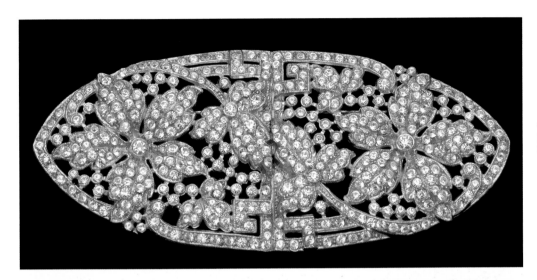

Art Deco brooch,
pot metal and clear
rhinestones, **$495**.

Birds in heart brooch, pot
metal and clear and green
rhinestones, red glass
cabochons, faux pearl,
$325.

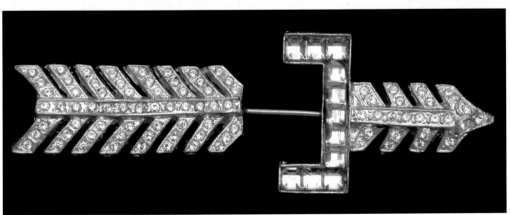

Arrow brooch, one side
screws off to open and
close the pin, pot metal
and clear rhinestones,
$115.

Flower brooch, pot metal and clear rhinestones, **$210**.

Leaf design brooch, pot metal and clear and blue rhinestones, **$185**.

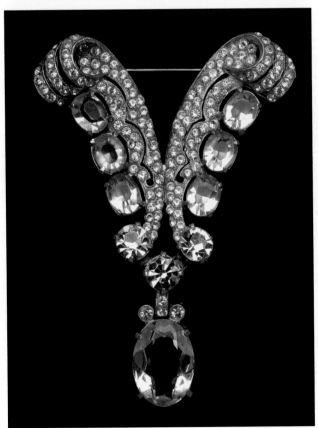

Salvo Art Deco brooch, pot metal and clear rhinestones, clear faceted glass, **$295**.

Artisan New York flower brooch, pot metal and clear rhinestones, faux pearls, **$165**.

Flower brooch, pot metal and clear rhinestones, **$185**.

Flower brooch, pot metal and clear rhinestones, **$265**.

Flower brooch, pot metal and clear rhinestones, clear faceted glass, **$180**.

Reinad flower brooch, rhodium and clear rhinestones, purple faceted glass, **$395**.

Flower brooch, rhodium and clear rhinestones, blue faceted glass, **$265**.

Flower brooch, pot metal and clear rhinestones, **$110**.

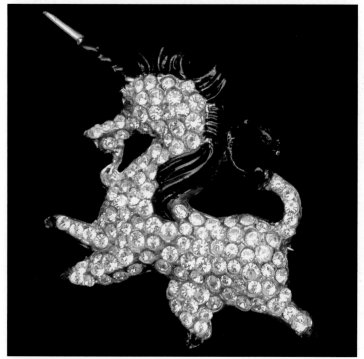

Schiaparelli unicorn brooch, pot metal and clear and green rhinestones, enameling, **$295**.

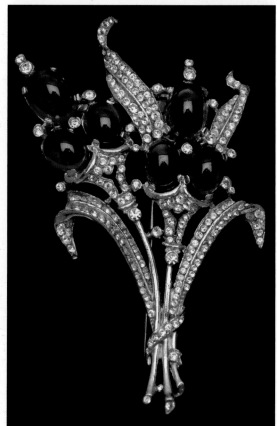

Flower brooch, pot metal and clear rhinestones, red glass cabochons, **$265**.

Peacock brooch, pot metal and clear, pink, blue, green, and citrine rhinestones, **$265**.

Pennino flower brooch, rhodium and clear rhinestones, purple faceted glass, enameling, **$345**.

Flower brooch, pot metal and clear rhinestones, enameling, **$110**.

Woman's face brooch, rhodium and clear, red, green, and blue rhinestones, **$265**.

Flower brooch, pot metal and clear rhinestones, red glass cabochons, **$165**.

Marcel Boucher grasshopper brooch, pot metal and clear rhinestones, enameling, **$950**.

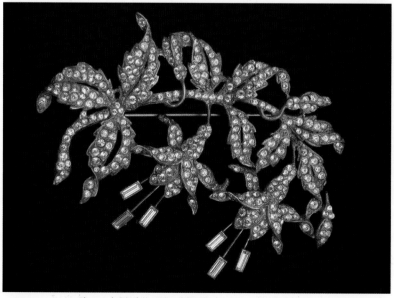

Flower brooch, pot metal and clear rhinestones, **$165**.

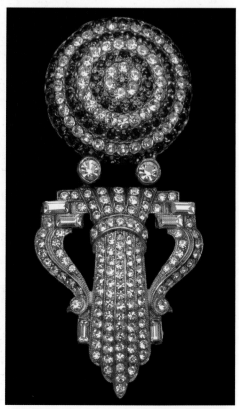

Art Deco brooch, pot metal and clear and blue rhinestones, **$185**.

Flower brooch, pot metal and clear rhinestones, **$155**.

Floral bouquet brooch, pot metal and clear rhinestones, **$195**.

Flower brooch, pot metal and clear rhinestones, enameling, **$145**.

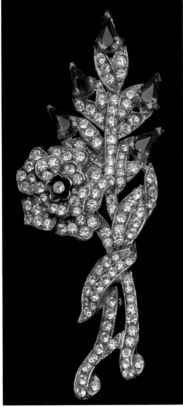

Flower brooch, pot metal and clear rhinestones, blue faceted glass, **$185**.

Flower brooch, pot metal and clear rhinestones, enameling, some wear to enamel, **$195**.

Flower brooch, pot metal and clear rhinestones, faux pearls, enameling, **$245**.

Flower brooch, pot metal and clear rhinestones, **$165**.

Three-dimensional flower brooch, pot metal and clear rhinestones, **$245**.

Corocraft flower brooch, sterling and clear and red rhinestones, **$225**.

Reja brooch, rhodium and clear rhinestones, faux pearls, **$345**.

Crown and heart brooch, pot metal and clear and green rhinestones, green glass cabochon, **$195**.

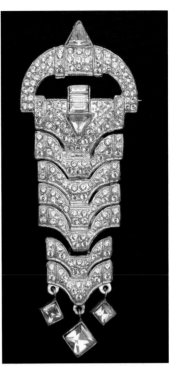

Art Deco buckle design brooch, pot metal and clear rhinestones, **$225**.

Flower brooch, pot metal and clear rhinestones, **$495**.

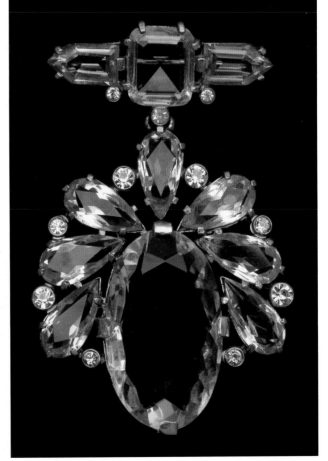

Art Deco brooch, pot metal and clear rhinestones, clear and blue faceted glass, **$450**.

Staret flower brooch, trembler, pot metal and clear rhinestones, **$395**.

Female skater brooch, pot metal and clear rhinestones, enameling, trembler flower, **$165**.

From left: fish brooch, pot metal and blue rhinestone, opalescent glass cabochons, enameling, **$65**; fish brooch, pot metal and clear and red rhinestones, blue glass cabochons, enameling, **$115**.

SEAFORD ADULT NON-FIC
Thu Nov 30 2023 01:05PM

Received. Belongs at SEAFORD
ADULT NON-FIC.

TITLE: Warman's vintage jewelry : identificatio
CALL NUMBER: 745.5942 L ;PA
BARCODE: 31835002803809
ITEM STATUS: IN TRANSIT
STAT GROUP: 20

From left: eagle brooch, pot metal and clear, red, and blue rhinestones, **$145**; eagle brooch, rhodium and clear and red rhinestones, **$225**.

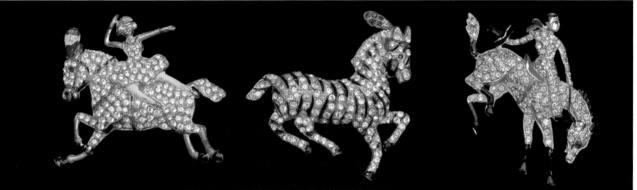

From left: lady riding horse brooch, pot metal and clear and red rhinestones, enameling, some wear to enamel, **$135**; dancing horse brooch, pot metal and clear and red rhinestones, enameling, some wear to enamel, **$165**; cowboy riding horse brooch, rhodium and clear rhinestones, enameling, **$135**.

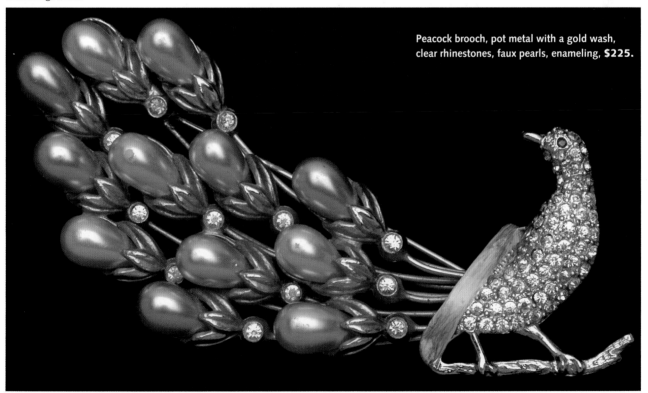

Peacock brooch, pot metal with a gold wash, clear rhinestones, faux pearls, enameling, **$225**.

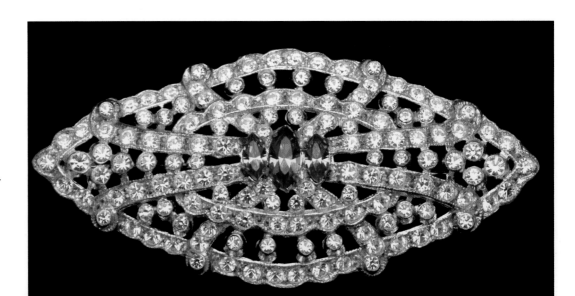

Art Deco brooch, pot metal and clear and blue rhinestones, **$110**.

Bow brooch, sterling and clear rhinestones, **$285**.

Bow brooch, pot metal and clear rhinestones, **$265**.

Flower brooch, trembler, pot metal and clear and green rhinestones, enameling, **$195**.

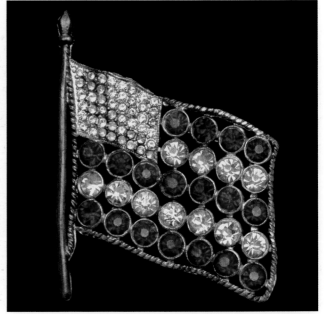

Flag brooch, pot metal and clear and red rhinestones, **$165**.

Art Deco brooch, pot metal and clear and blue rhinestones, **$195**.

From left: flower brooch, pot metal and clear and purple rhinestones, **$185**; flower brooch, pot metal and clear and green rhinestones, **$225**.

Flower brooch, pot metal and clear rhinestones, pink glass cabochons, enameling, wear to enameling, **$165**.

From left: flower brooch, pot metal and clear and blue rhinestones, **$195**; flower brooch, pot metal and clear, red, green, and blue rhinestones, **$195**.

Flower brooch, pot metal and clear rhinestones, blue glass cabochons, enameling, **$155**.

Staret rooster brooch, pot metal and clear rhinestones, enameling, **$265.**

Rooster brooch, pot me.tal and clear rhinestones, enameling, some wear to enamel, **$110**.

Circus horse brooch, rhodium and clear rhinestones, enameling, **$245.**

From left: Coro dog brooches, pot metal and clear rhinestones, tan molded glass, **$165**; pot metal and clear rhinestones, blue molded glass, **$185**.

Eagle brooch, pot metal and clear rhinestones, enameling, **$295**.

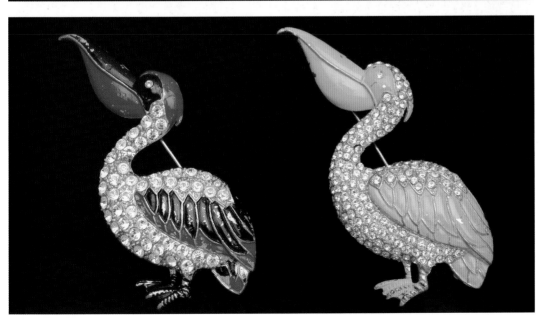

From left: pelican brooch, pot metal and clear rhinestones, enameling, some wear to enamel, **$295**; pelican brooch, pot metal and clear rhinestones, enameling, some wear to enamel, **$295**.

Art Deco bow brooch, rhodium and clear, red, green, and blue rhinestones, **$195**.

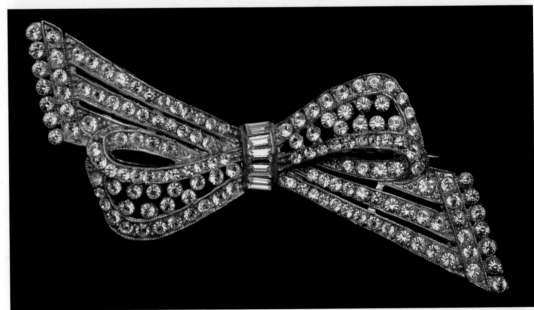

Bow brooch, rhodium and clear rhinestones, **$145**.

Art Deco brooch, pot metal and clear rhinestones, **$165**.

Art Deco brooch, pot metal and clear and blue rhinestones, blue faceted glass, enameling, **$245**.

Bow brooch, pot metal and clear rhinestones, **$95**.

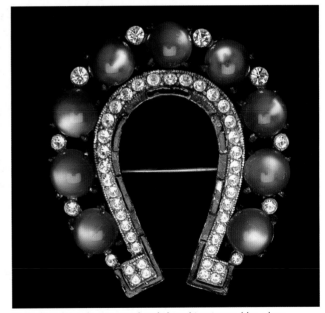

Horseshoe brooch, pot metal and clear rhinestones, blue glass cabochons, enameling, **$110**.

Art Deco brooch, pot metal and clear and citrine rhinestones, citrine faceted glass, **$90**.

Art Deco brooch, pot metal and clear rhinestones, amethyst-colored faceted glass, **$175**.

Natty Creations scarf holder brooch, pot metal and clear, blue, red, and green rhinestones, **$110**.

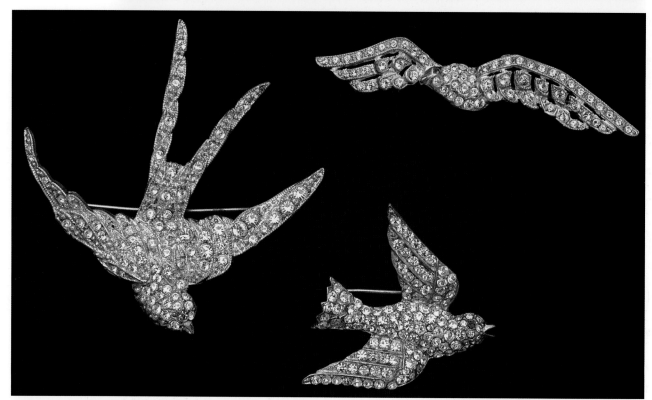

Clockwise from left: bird brooch, pot metal and clear and blue rhinestones, **$98**; bird brooch, pot metal and clear and red rhinestones, **$88**; Corocraft bird brooch, sterling and clear and red rhinestones, **$165**.

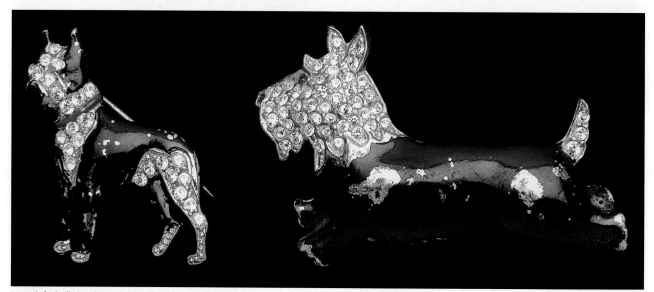

From left: bull dog brooch, rhodium and clear rhinestones, enameling, some wear to enamel, **$88**; dog brooch, rhodium and clear and red rhinestones, enameling, some wear to enamel, **$135**.

Natty Creations scarf holder brooch, pot metal and clear rhinestones, missing one stone, **$95**.

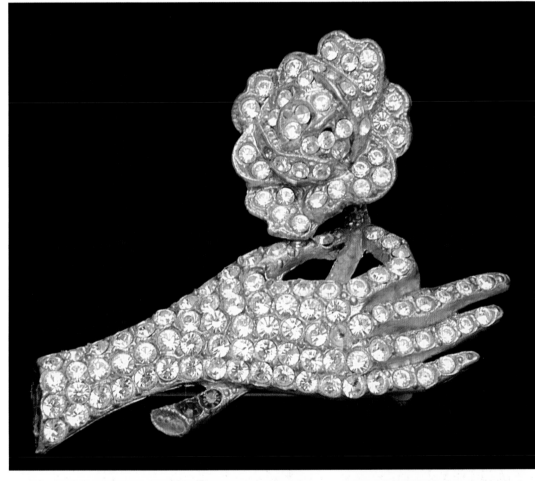

Hand and flower brooch, trembler, pot metal and rhinestones, enameling, **$145**.

Flower brooch, pot metal and marcasites, blue faceted glass, **$155**.

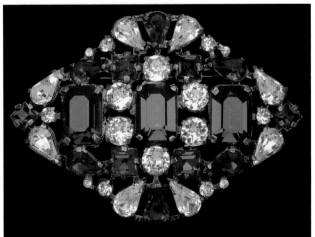

Brooch, pot metal and clear and green rhinestones, **$155**.

121

Flower brooches, pot metal and clear rhinestones, **$165** each.

Below: sailfish brooches, pot metal and clear and red rhinestones, enameling, **$95** each.

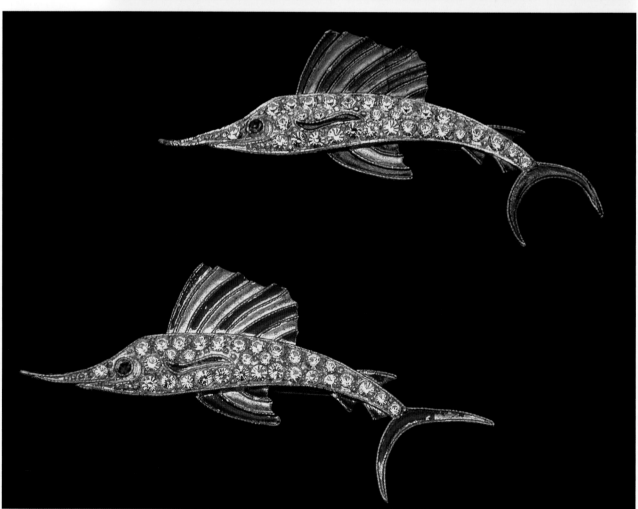

Bow brooches, pot metal and clear rhinestones, **$125** each.

Below: sailfish brooches, pot metal and clear and red rhinestones, enameling, **$115** each.

Fish brooches, pot metal and clear rhinestones, enameling; from top left clockwise: **$110**, **$95**, **$125**.

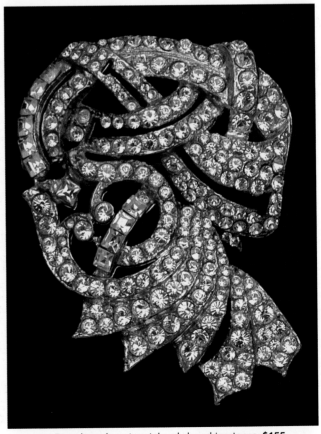

Fish brooch, rhodium and clear rhinestones, red cabochon, enameling, **$165**.

Art Deco brooch, pot metal and clear rhinestones, **$155**.

Lizard brooches, pot metal and clear and green rhinestones, enameling, **$175** each.

Squirrel brooch, pot metal and clear rhinestones, enameling, **$195**.

Bird brooch, pot metal and clear and red rhinestones, enameling, **$110**.

Saxophone brooch, pot metal and clear rhinestones, enameling, **$64**.

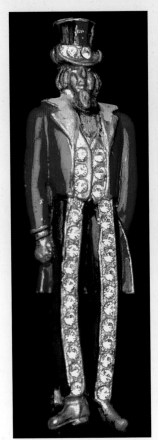

Patriotic brooches, clockwise from left: Uncle Sam pin, pot metal and clear rhinestones, enameling, some wear to enamel, **$185**; "V" for victory tie tack, pot metal and clear, red, and blue rhinestones, **$65**; eagle pin, rhodium and red, clear, and blue rhinestones, enameling, **$125**.

Bird brooch, pot metal and clear and red rhinestones, enameling, **$68**.

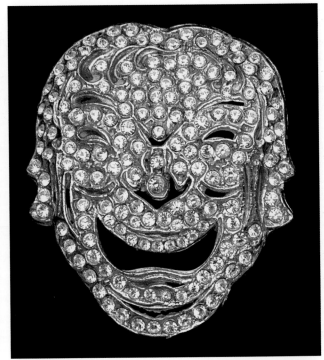

AJ laughing face brooch, pot metal and clear rhinestones, **$140**.

Flower brooch, rhodium and clear rhinestones, purple faceted glass, **$185**; flower brooch, rhodium and clear rhinestones, citrine faceted glass, **$185**.

From left: flower bouquet brooch, pot metal and clear, green, pink, and blue rhinestones, enameling, **$65**; flower bouquet brooch, pot metal and clear and blue rhinestones, enameling, **$85**.

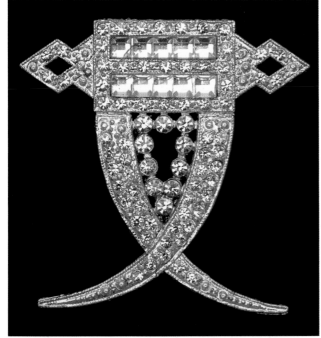

Art Deco brooch, pot metal and clear rhinestones, **$80**.

Bow brooch, pot metal and clear rhinestones, red glass cabochon, enameling, **$110**.

Leaf brooch, rhodium and clear rhinestones, **$110**.

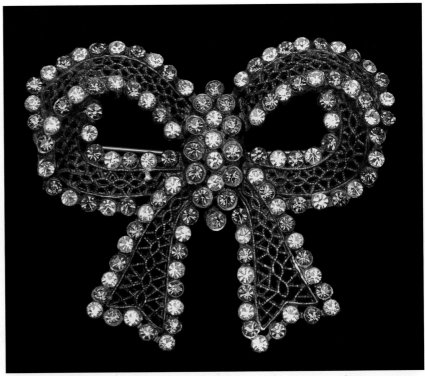

Filligree bow brooch, pot metal and clear and blue rhinestones, **$155**.

Flower brooch, pot metal and clear rhinestones, blue faceted glass, **$68**.

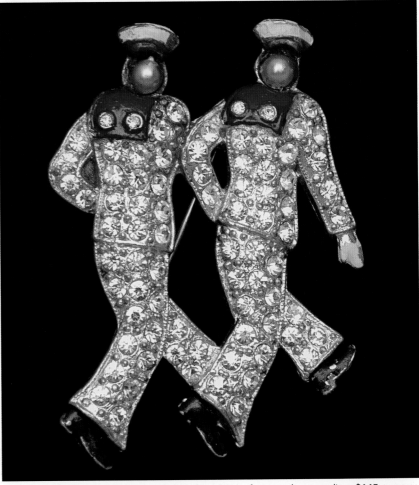

Sailor brooch, pot metal and clear rhinestones, faux pearls, enameling, **$145**.

From top: double bird brooch, rhodium and clear rhinestones, enameling, wear to enamel, **$195**; bird brooch, pot metal and clear and green rhinestones, enameling, wear to enamel, **$135**.

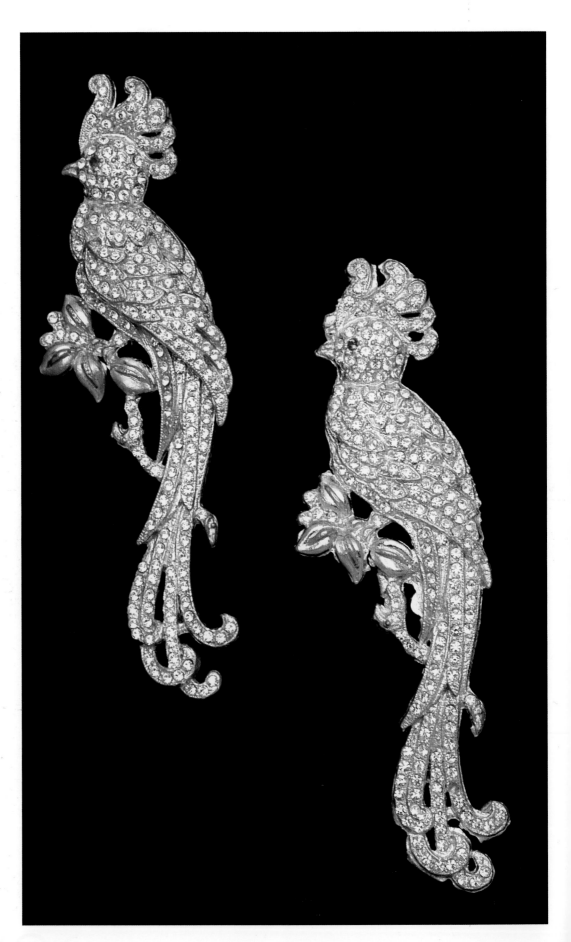

Cockatoo brooches, pot metal and clear rhinestones, **$185** each.

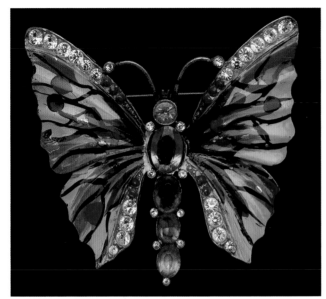

Butterfly brooch, pot metal and clear, citrine, red, and blue rhinestones, enameling, **$145**.

Flower brooch, trembler, pot metal and clear and red rhinestones, **$195**.

Butterfly brooch, pot metal and clear rhinestones, red and green glass cabochons, **$185**.

Butterfly brooch, pot metal and clear and green rhinestones, clear faceted glass, **$285**.

Butterfly brooch, pot metal and clear, green and red rhinestones, **$285**.

Butterfly brooch, pot metal and clear and blue rhinestones, blue faceted glass, **$285**.

Peacock brooch, pot metal and clear rhinestones, faux pearls, enameling, some wear to enamel, faux pearls have been replaced with contemporary faux pearls, **$155**.

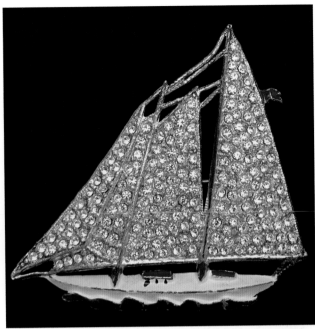

Sailboat brooch, pot metal and clear rhinestones, enameling, **$135**.

Basket brooch, pot metal and clear rhinestones, pink glass cabochons, enameling, **$145**.

Bow brooch, pot metal and clear rhinestones, **$165**.

Bow brooch, pot metal and clear rhinestones, **$155**.

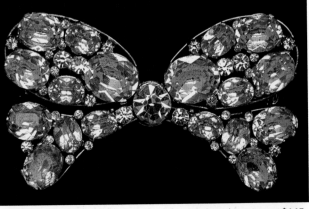

Czechoslovakian bow brooch, pot metal and clear rhinestones, **$145**.

Bird brooch, pot metal and clear rhinestones, **$115**.

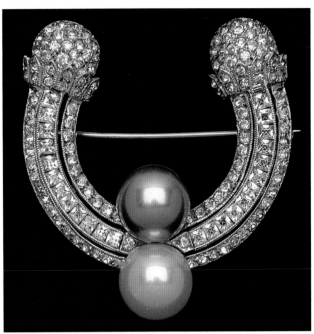

Art Deco brooch, rhodium and clear rhinestones, faux pearls, **$225**.

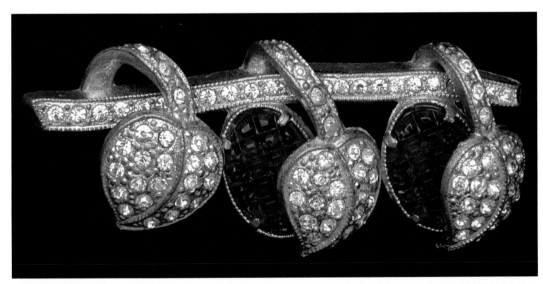

Leaf brooch, pot metal and clear rhinestones, molded glass, **$115**.

Jay flower brooch, pot metal and clear rhinestones, molded glass, **$125**.

Fish brooch, pot metal and clear rhinestones, enameling, faux pearls, **$155**.

Fish brooch, pot metal and clear rhinestones, enameling, **$110**.

Silson bird brooch, pot metal and clear rhinestones, faux pearl, enameling, some wear to enamel, **$195**.

Double bird brooch, pot metal and clear rhinestones, faux pearls, enameling, **$165**.

Fish brooch, pot metal and clear and blue rhinestones, molded glass, enameling, **$145**.

Art Deco brooch, pot metal and clear rhinestones, blue glass cabochons, **$125**.

Czechoslovakian Art Deco brooch, pot metal and red, citrine, green, blue, and amethyst rhinestones, **$95**.

Floral brooch, pot metal and clear rhinestones, blue faceted glass, **$155**.

Czechoslovakian brooch, pot metal and blue rhinestones, **$65**.

Flower brooch, pot metal and clear and green rhinestones, **$195**.

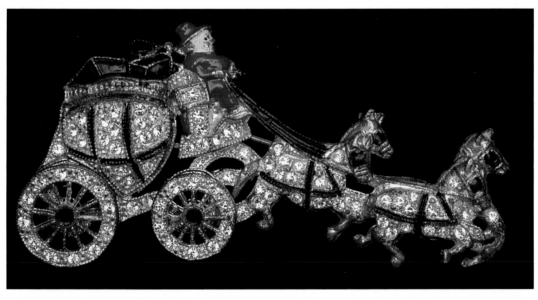

Horse and coachman brooch, pot metal and clear rhinestones, enameling, wheels move, **$145**.

Bow brooch, pot metal and clear rhinestones, **$165**.

Alligator brooch, pot metal and clear and green rhinestones, green faceted glass, **$125**.

Rooster brooch, pot metal and clear, red, and green rhinestones, **$165**.

Bird brooch, pot metal and clear and red rhinestones, **$195**.

Turtle brooch, pot metal and clear and red rhinestones, **$135**.

Coro Scottie dog brooch, pot metal and clear rhinestones, molded glass, **$185**.

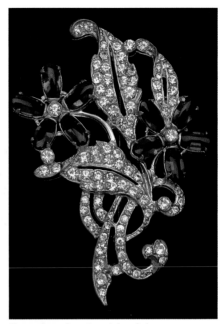

Rickshaw brooch, pot metal and clear rhinestones, red cabochon, enameling, wheels move, **$180**.

Flower brooch, pot metal and clear rhinestones, faceted blue glass, **$110**.

Czechoslovakian flower brooch, pot metal and clear rhinestones, **$165**.

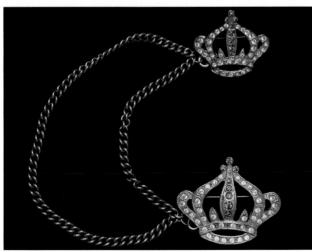

Double crown brooch with chains, pot metal and clear and blue rhinestones, **$88**.

Bug brooch, sterling and clear, pink, and green rhinestones, enameling, wear to enamel, **$185**.

Double bird brooch, pot metal and clear and pink rhinestones, faux pearls, enameling, **$185**.

Boucher double bird brooch, rhodium and clear and red rhinestones, faux pearls, **$225**.

Airplane brooch, pot metal and clear rhinestones, enameling, wear to enamel, **$145**.

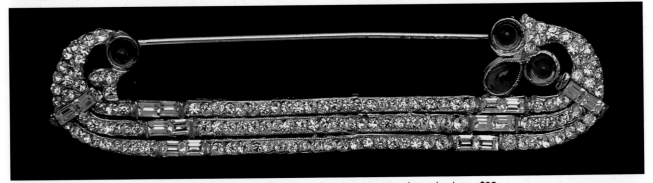

Art Deco brooch, pot metal and clear rhinestones, green glass cabochons, **$98**.

Covered wagon brooch, pot metal and clear rhinestones, enameling, wheels move, **$115**.

Owl brooch, pot metal and clear rhinestones, enameling, **$185**.

Bird brooch, pot metal and clear and red rhinestones, **$155**.

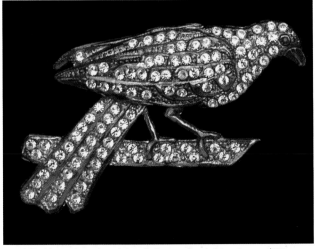

Bird brooch, pot metal and clear and red rhinestones, **$85**.

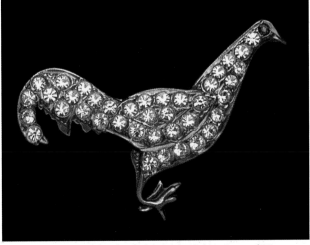

Bird pin, pot metal and clear and red rhinestones, **$85**.

Bow brooch, pot metal and clear rhinestones, **$145**.

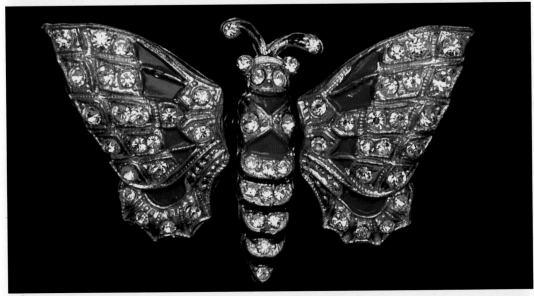

Butterfly brooch, trembling wings, pot metal and clear rhinestones, enameling, **$145**.

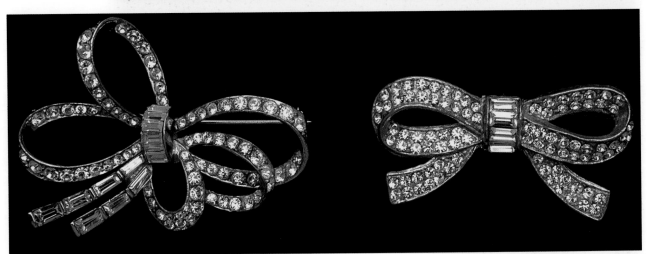

Boucher bow brooch, rhodium and clear rhinestones, **$125**; bow brooch, pot metal and clear rhinestones, **$95**.

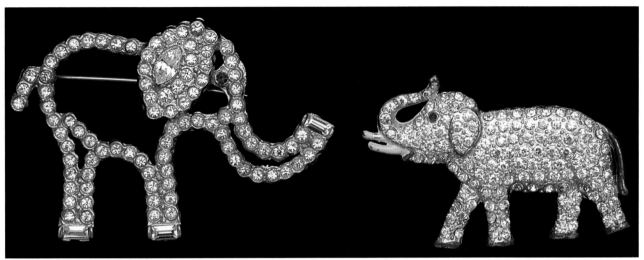

Elephant brooch, pot metal and clear and red rhinestones, **$95**; elephant brooch, pot metal and clear and red rhinestones, enameling, **$125**.

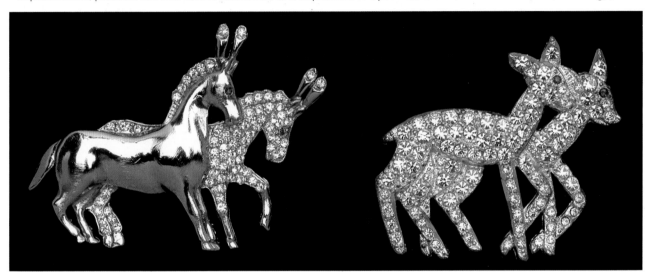

Double horse brooch, pot metal and clear and red rhinestones, **$95**; double deer brooch, pot metal and clear, red, and green rhinestones, **$85**.

Bow brooch, pot metal and clear rhinestones, **$365**.

Brooch, sterling and clear rhinestones, blue and opalescent glass cabochons, **$245**.

Floral brooch, pot metal and clear rhinestones, faceted pink glass, **$190**.

Grape brooch, pot metal and clear, red, green, blue, and purple rhinestones, **$45**.

Leaf brooch, rhodium and clear rhinestones, **$115**.

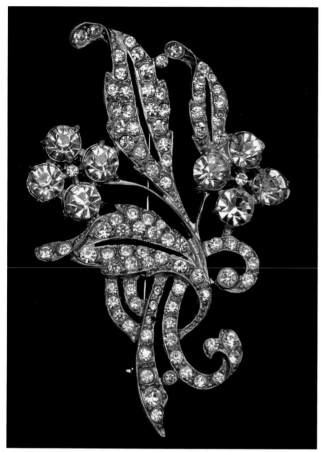

Flower brooch, pot metal and clear rhinestones, **$95**.

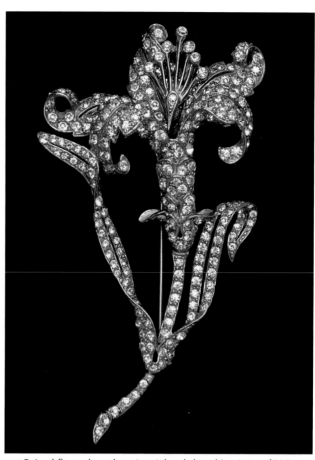

Reinad flower brooch, pot metal and clear rhinestones, **$295**.

Flower brooch, pot metal and clear rhinestones, **$165**.

Floral brooch, rhodium and clear rhinestones, blue glass cabochons, enameling, **$225**.

Corocraft cockatoo brooch, rhodium and clear and blue rhinestones, enameling, **$325**.

Bird brooch, pot metal and clear and red rhinestones, enameling, **$185**.

Bird brooch, pot metal and clear and red rhinestones, enameling, **$135**.

Flower brooch, pot metal and clear rhinestones, enameling, some wear to enamel, **$125**.

Trifari flower brooch, pot metal and clear rhinestones, faceted blue glass, enameling, **$225**.

Bird brooch, pot metal and clear rhinestones, enameling, **$125**.

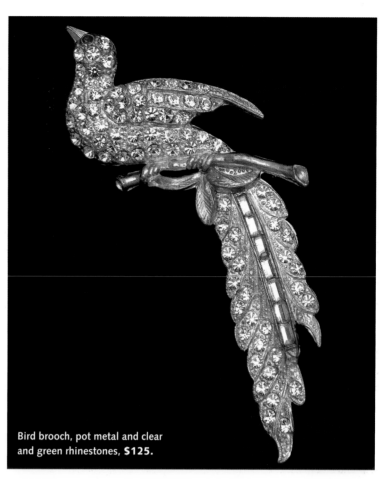

Bird brooch, pot metal and clear and green rhinestones, **$125.**

Bird brooch, pot metal and clear and red rhinestones, enameling, some wear to enamel, **$185**.

Bird brooch, pot metal and clear and green rhinestones, **$145**.

Bug brooch, pot metal and clear rhinestones, green faceted glass, **$155**.

Stork brooch, pot metal and clear and red rhinestones, **$90**.

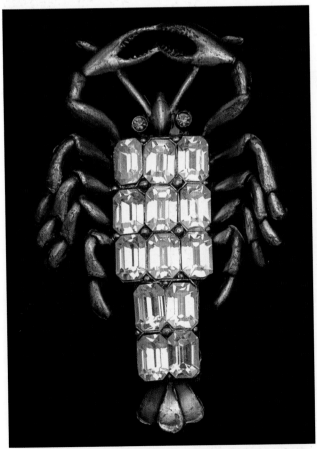

Scorpion brooch, pot metal and clear and green rhinestones, **$110**.

Owl brooch, pot metal and clear and citrine rhinestones, enameling, **$165**.

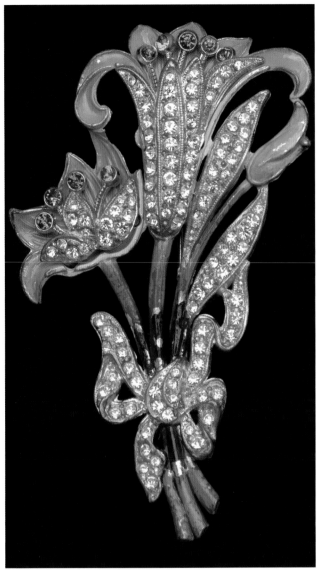

Flower brooch, pot metal and clear, green, blue, pink, and citrine rhinestones, enameling, wear to enamel, **$175**.

Flower brooch, rhodium and clear and red rhinestones, **$195**.

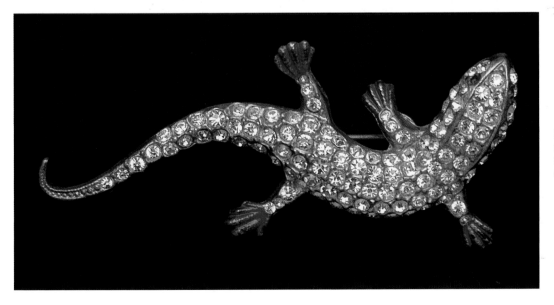

Lizard brooch, pot metal and clear and red rhinestones, enameling, **$175**.

Eagle brooch, pot metal and clear rhinestones, enameling, **$185**.

Wishing well brooch, pot metal and clear, green, red, and blue rhinestones, enameling, **$125**.

Bird brooches, pot metal and clear rhinestones, **$115** each.

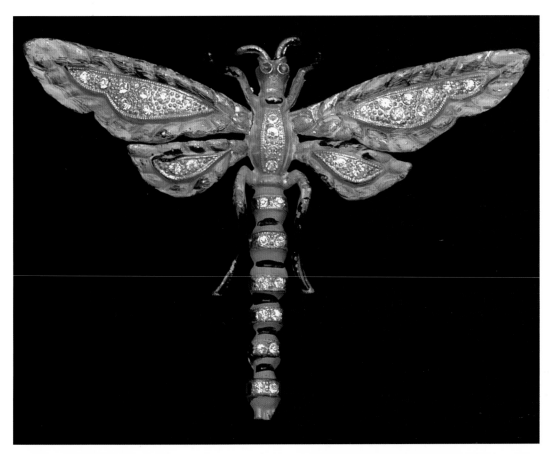

Dragonfly brooch, pot metal and clear and red rhinestones, enameling, **$165**.

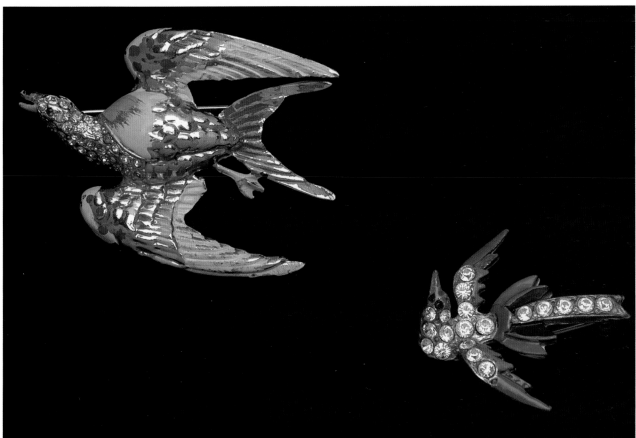

From left: bird brooch, rhodium and clear rhinestones, enameling, **$110**; bird brooch, pot metal and clear rhinestones, enameling, **$70**.

Eisenberg eagle brooch with clear rhinestones, enameling, **$650**.

Reinad bug brooch with clear, blue, and pink rhinestones, **$325**.

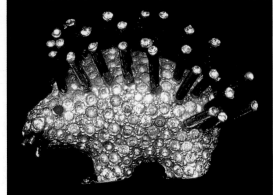

Porcupine brooch, pot metal and clear and red rhinestones, enameling, **$145**.

Pear brooch, pot metal and clear rhinestones, enameling, **$110**.

Mazer brooch, pot metal and clear rhinestones, **$180**.

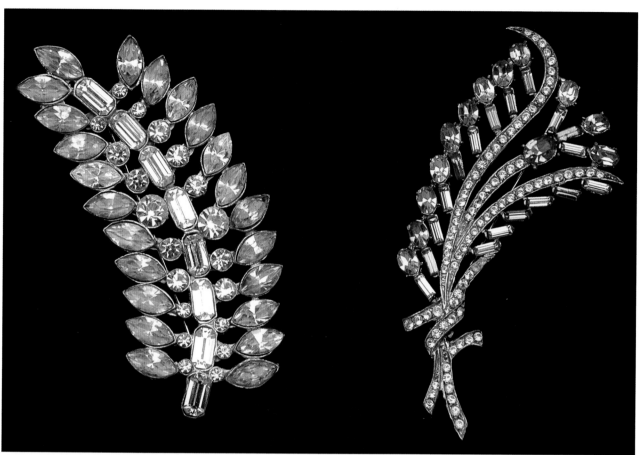

From left: leaf brooch, pot metal and clear rhinestones, **$48**; leaf brooch, pot metal and clear, pink, citrine, blue, and green rhinestones, **$130**.

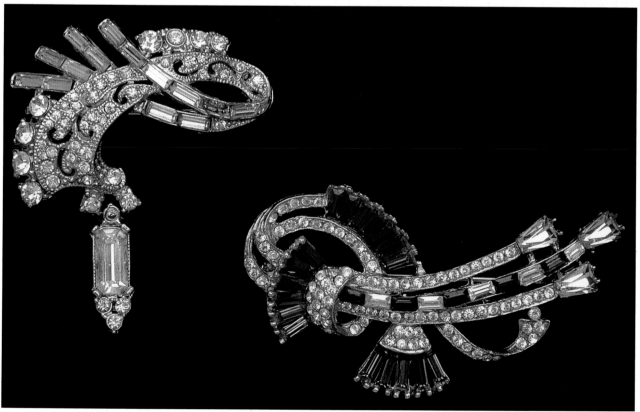

From left: brooch, pot metal and clear rhinestones, **$75**; brooch, rhodium and clear and blue rhinestones, **$145**.

Left: Staret floral brooch, pot metal and clear rhinestones, **$195**. Middle: floral brooch, pot metal and clear and pink rhinestones, **$125**. Right: floral brooch, rhodium and clear rhinestones, **$90**.

Left: Coro flower brooch, trembler, pot metal and clear and lavender rhinestones, enameling, **$165**. Middle: Staret floral brooch, pot metal and clear rhinestones, faux pearl, **$275**. Right: flower brooch, trembler, pot metal and clear rhinestones, glass beads, **$95**.

Top left: Eisenberg Original bow brooch, pot metal and clear rhinestones, **$385**. Top right: bow brooch, pot metal and clear rhinestones, **$225**. Bottom: Eisenberg Original bow brooch, pot metal and clear rhinestones, **$345**.

Left: Staret floral brooch, pot metal and clear rhinestones, enameling, **$390**. Right: floral brooch, pot metal and clear rhinestones, enameling, **$45**.

Staret brooch, rhodium and clear rhinestones, green faceted glass, **$745**.

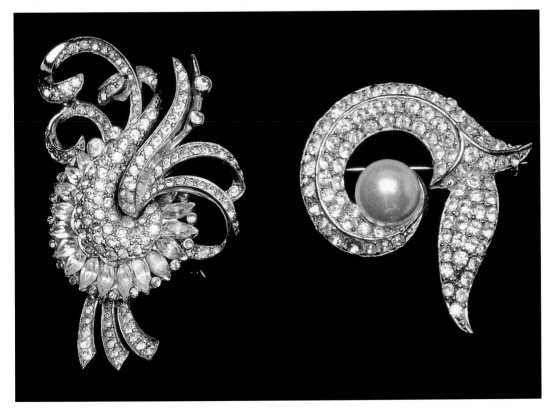

Left: Jomaz brooch, rhodium and clear rhinestones, **$185**. Right: Ledo brooch, pot metal and clear rhinestones, faux pearl, **$60**.

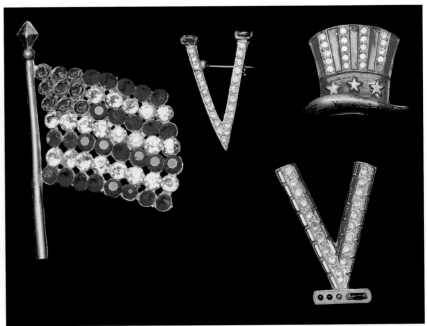

Left: flag brooch, pot metal and clear, red, and blue rhinestones, **$145**. Top middle: victory brooch, pot metal and clear, red, and blue rhinestones, **$65**. Bottom middle: victory brooch, pot metal and clear rhinestones and red and blue enameling, **$60**. Right: Uncle Sam hat brooch, pot metal and clear rhinestones, enameling, **$95**.

Top: Trifari crown brooch with clear, red, blue, and green rhinestones, **$155**. Middle: Corocraft three-dimensional crown brooch with clear rhinestones, **$185**. Bottom: Corocraft crown brooch, sterling and clear rhinestones, **$145**.

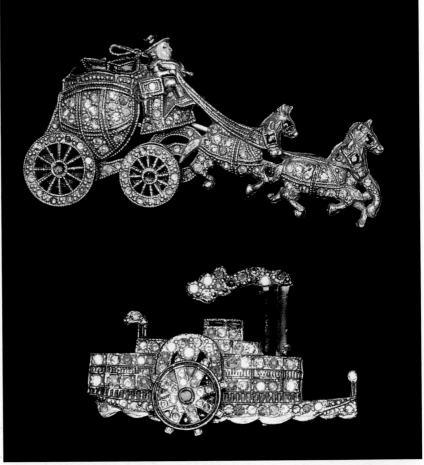

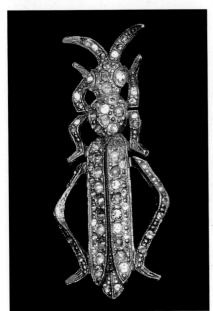

Bug brooch, pot metal and clear, topaz, green, pink, and blue rhinestones, **$65**.

Top: horse and carriage brooch, pot metal and pink, blue, green, topaz, and amethyst rhinestones, **$95**. Bottom: steamboat brooch, pot metal and clear, blue, topaz, green, pink, and amethyst rhinestones, **$95**.

Left: floral brooch, pot metal and clear rhinestones, enameling, **$145**. Top: flower brooch, pot metal and clear rhinestones, enameling, **$185**. Right: flower brooch, trembler, pot metal and clear rhinestones, pink cabochons, enameling, **$155**.

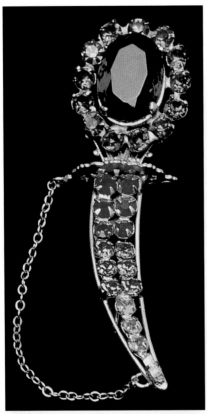

Sword brooch, rhodium and green, amethyst, red, blue and topaz rhinestones, **$85**.

Corocraft jelly belly fish brooch, sterling and clear and pink rhinestones, enameling, **$495**.

Coro flamingo brooch, pot metal and clear rhinestones, enameling, **$295**. Top right: Jomaz mallard brooch, rhodium and clear rhinestones and enameling, **$145**. Bottom right: Grasshopper brooch, pot metal and clear rhinestones, enameling, **$95**.

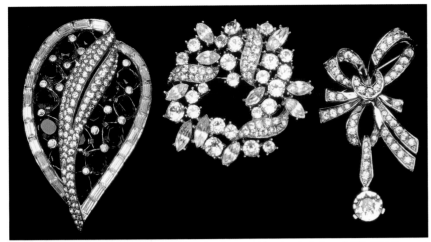

Left: Jomaz leaf brooch, rhodium and clear rhinestones, blue faceted glass, **$135**. Middle: Trifari brooch, rhodium and clear rhinestones, **$45**. Right: Boucher bow brooch, rhodium and clear rhinestones, **$125**.

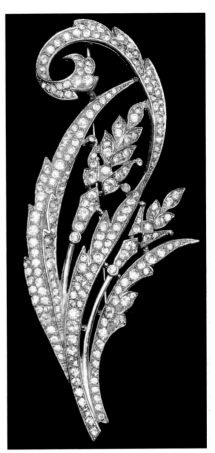

Trifari floral brooch, rhodium with clear rhinestones, **$185**.

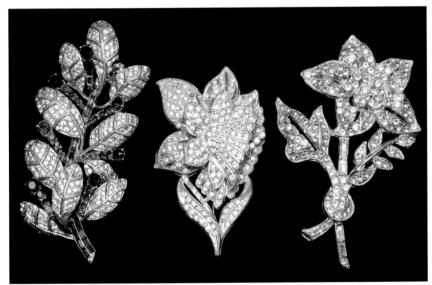

Left: floral brooch, pot metal and clear and green rhinestones, **$165**. Middle: floral brooch, pot metal and clear rhinestones, **$125**. Right: floral brooch, pot metal and clear rhinestones, **$110**.

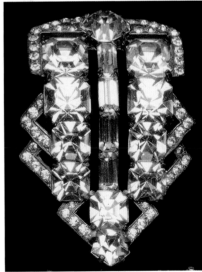

Eisenberg Original brooch with clear rhinestones, **$395**.

Left: flower basket brooch, pot metal and clear rhinestones and green, blue, yellow, and burgundy cabochons, **$58**. Middle: Leo Glass floral arrangement brooch with clear, green, blue, pink, topaz, and amethyst rhinestones, **$165**. Right: floral basket brooch, pot metal and blue rhinestones, faux turquoise cabochons, **$62**.

Flower bouquet brooch, pot metal and green rhinestones, molded glass leaves, **$65**.

Berry brooch, pot metal and clear rhinestones and glass beads, **$135**.

Top: bow brooch, pot metal and clear faceted glass, blue cabochons, **$265**. Bottom: brooch, pot metal and clear rhinestones, **$90**.

Floral bouquet brooch, pot metal and blue rhinestones, enameling, **$145**.

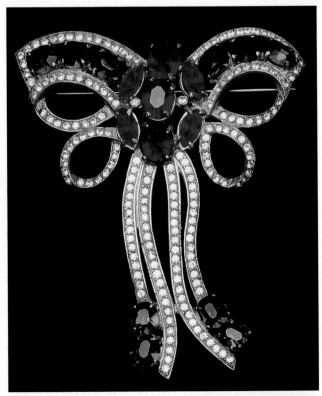

Eisenberg Original bow brooch, clear, red and amethyst rhinestones, **$545**.

Enameled floral brooch, rhodium and marcasites, **$145**.

Enameled floral brooch, sterling and marcasites, **$195**.

Floral brooch, rhodium and clear rhinestones, glass beads, enameling, **$245**.

Brooch, rhodium and clear and red rhinestones, **$165**.

Eisenberg Original brooch, sterling and clear rhinestones, **$450**.

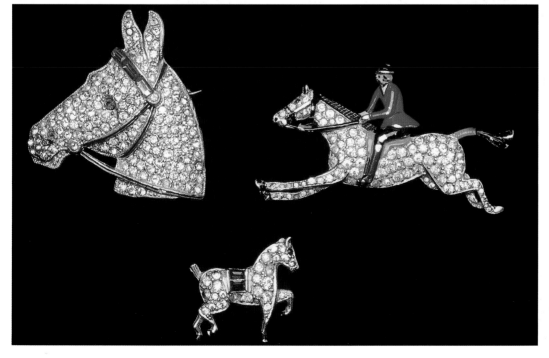

Top left: horse head brooch, pot metal and clear, blue and green rhinestones, **$110**. Top right: Trifari horse and jockey brooch, pot metal and clear rhinestones, enameling, **$125**. Bottom: Trifari horse pin, pot metal and clear and blue rhinestones, **$45**.

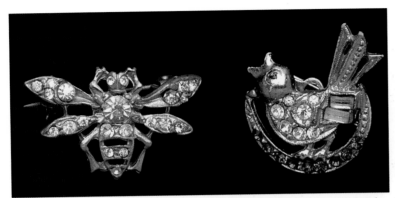

From left: fly pin, pot metal and clear rhinestones, **$24**; chirping bird pin, pot metal and clear and blue rhinestones, **$30**.

Floral brooch, pot metal and clear rhinestones, enameling, **$95**.

Staret brooch with clear rhinestones, **$325**.

Jomaz floral brooch, rhodium and clear, red, and blue rhinestones, **$85**.

Pair of leaf design pins, pot metal and clear and green rhinestones, **$225**.

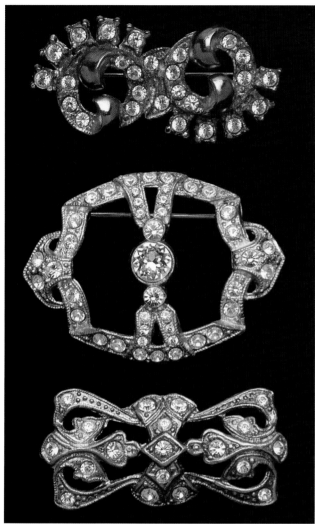

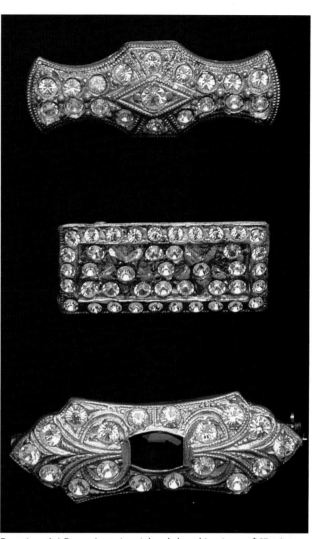

From top: pin, pot metal and clear rhinestones, **$28**; Art Deco pin, pot metal and clear rhinestones, **$55**; Art Deco pin, pot metal and clear rhinestones, **$32**.

From top: Art Deco pin, pot metal and clear rhinestones, **$65**; pin, pot metal and clear rhinestones, **$42**; Art Deco pin, pot metal and clear and blue rhinestones, **$65**.

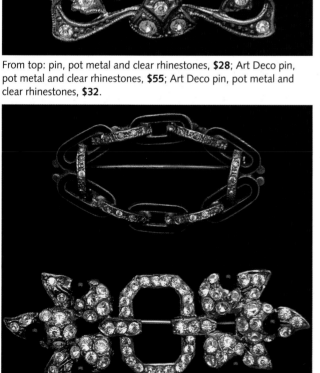

From top: Art Deco pin, pot metal and clear rhinestones, enameling, **$48**; Art Deco brooch, pot metal and clear rhinestones, black glass beads, **$168**.

Ora bird brooch, pot metal and clear rhinestones, **$55**.

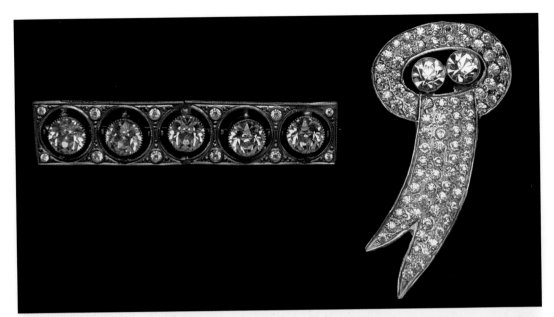

From left: bar pin, pot metal and clear rhinestones, **$85**; Art Deco brooch, pot metal and clear rhinestones, **$95**.

From left: Coro elephant pin, pot metal and clear rhinestones, enameling, some wear to enamel, **$95**; rooster pin, pot metal and clear rhinestones, enameling, **$65**.

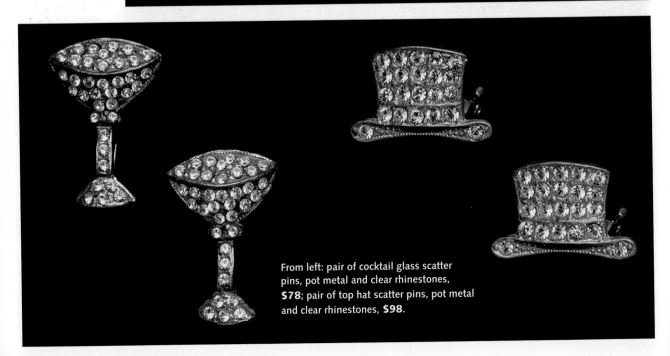

From left: pair of cocktail glass scatter pins, pot metal and clear rhinestones, **$78**; pair of top hat scatter pins, pot metal and clear rhinestones, **$98**.

Rotary floral watch pin, rhodium and clear rhinestones, faceted blue glass, **$425**.

Below from top: Art Deco bar pin, sterling and blue and clear rhinestones, **$85**; Art Deco bar pin; sterling and clear and blue rhinestones, **$95**.

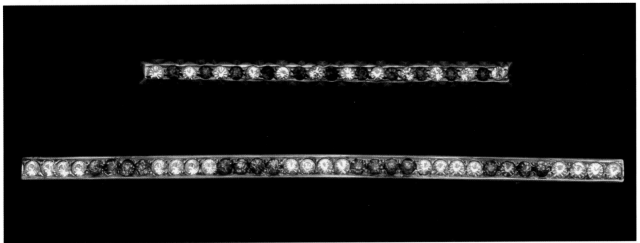

From left: flower bouquet pin, pot metal and clear rhinestones, **$48**; floral bouquet pin, pot metal and clear rhinestones, **$32**.

From left: pin, pot metal and clear rhinestones, **$16**; pin, pot metal and clear rhinestones, **$28**.

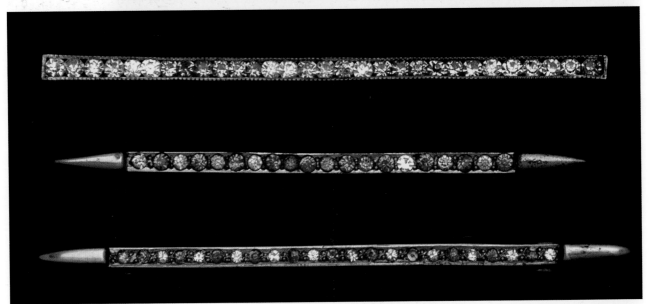

From top: Art Deco bar pin, sterling and clear and blue rhinestones, **$85**; Art Deco bar pin, sterling and green and clear rhinestones, **$85**; Art Deco bar pin, sterling and blue and clear rhinestones, **$85**.

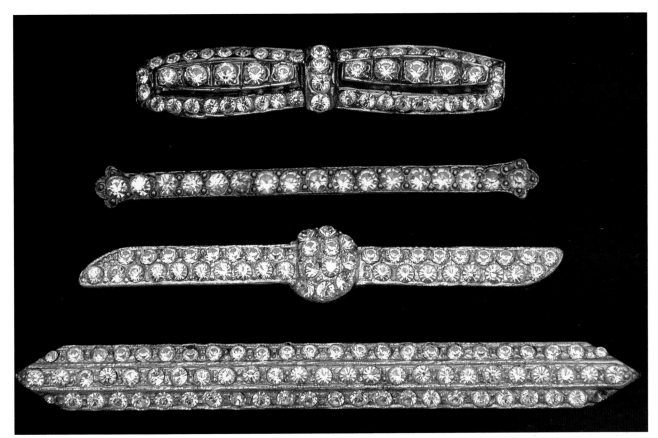

From top: Art Deco brooch, pot metal and clear rhinestones, **$85**; Art Deco bar pin, pot metal and clear rhinestones, **$28**; Art Deco bar pin, pot metal and clear rhinestones, **$45**; Art Deco bar pin, pot metal and clear rhinestones, **$58**.

Taft presidential pin, pot metal and clear rhinestones, **$42**.

Frog pin, pot metal and clear and green rhinestones, **$45**.

Owl pin, pot metal and clear and green rhinestones, **$68**.

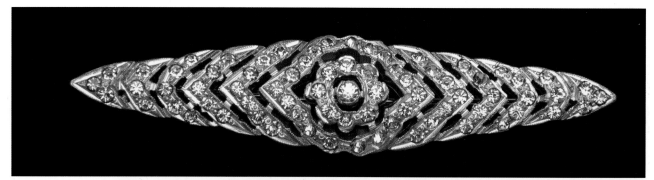

Bar pin, pot metal and clear rhinestones, **$85**.

Front and back views of lady watch pin, pot metal and clear, red, citrine, blue, and green rhinestones, enameling, **$345**.

Right: Wishing well pin, pot metal and clear, red, pink and blue rhinestones, **$95**.

Far right: Buddha pin, sterling and clear rhinestones, green molded glass, **$85**.

Harvey fish watch pin, pot metal and clear rhinestones, green cabochons, enameling, **$395**.

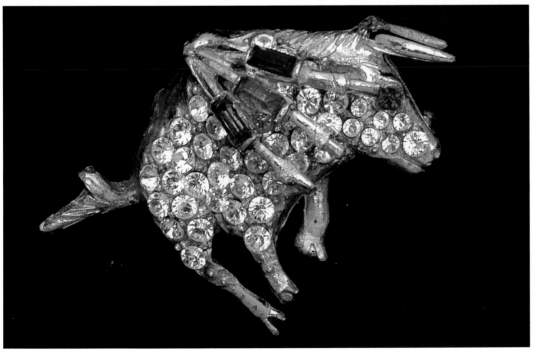

Pell bull pin, pot metal and clear, blue, green, red, and pink rhinestones, **$85**.

Clips

Trifari fur clip, rhodium and clear rhinestones, green faceted glass, enameling, **$425**.

Pair of Eisenberg Original dress clips, pot metal and clear rhinestones, **$145**.

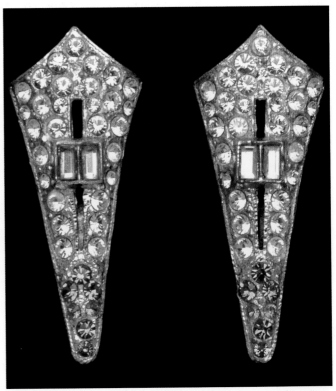

Pair of Art Deco dress clips, pot metal and clear and blue rhinestones, **$95**.

Pair of bow dress clips, pot metal and rhinestones, **$385**.

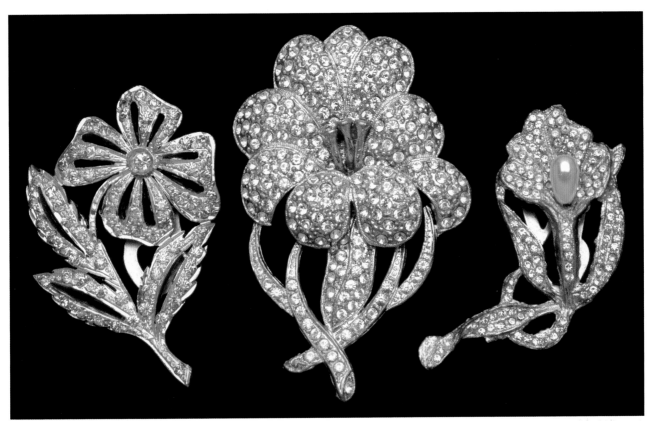

From left: flower dress clip, rhodium and clear rhinestones, **$88**; flower dress clip, pot metal and clear rhinestones, **$195**; flower dress clip, pot metal and clear rhinestones, **$45**.

Pair of dress clips, pot metal and clear and blue rhinestones, **$95**.

Grape design fur clip, pot metal and clear rhinestones, moonglow cabochons, enameling, **$135**.

From left: buckle design dress clip, pot metal and clear and red rhinestones, **$45**; Art Deco dress clip, pot metal and red and clear rhinestones, **$110**; Art Deco dress clip, pot metal and red and clear rhinestones, **$32**.

Swiss man fur clip, pot metal and clear rhinestones, enameling, **$110**.

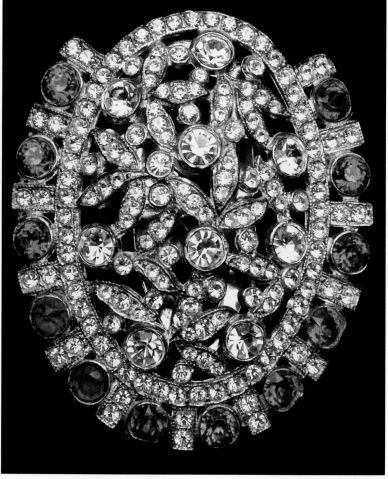

Dress clip, pot metal and clear and red rhinestones, **$125**.

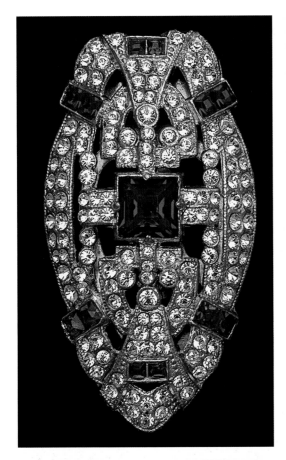

Art Deco dress clip, pot metal and clear and red rhinestones, **$135**; Art Deco dress clip, pot metal and clear and green rhinestones, **$135**.

Trifari fur clip with red and clear rhinestones, enameling, **$345**.

Master Craft dress clip, pot metal and clear rhinestones, blue, red, green, and citrine faceted glass, **$165**.

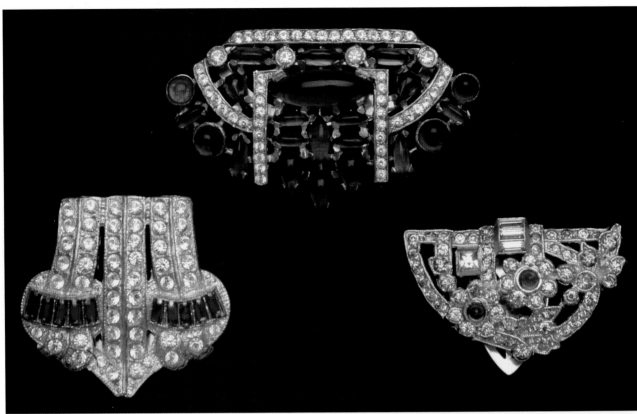

Above from left: Art Deco dress clip, pot metal and clear and green rhinestones, **$68**; Art Deco dress clip, pot metal and clear rhinestones, green cabochons, **$125**; floral design dress clip, rhodium and clear rhinestones, green cabochons, **$48**.

Pair of Art Deco dress clips, pot metal and clear and green rhinestones, **$125**.

Floral design dress clip, pot metal and clear rhinestones, green cabochon, **$85**.

Flower dress clip, pot metal and clear and green rhinestones, **$98**.

Art Deco dress clip, pot metal and clear and green rhinestones, **$145**.

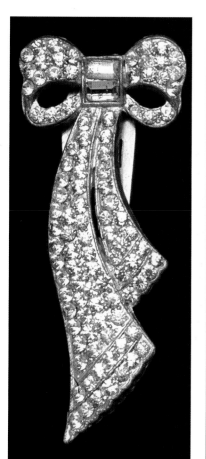

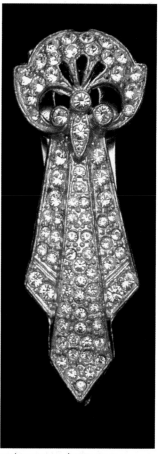

From left: bow design dress clip, pot metal and clear rhinestones, **$78**; Art Deco dress clip, pot metal and clear rhinestones, **$110**; Art Deco dress clip, pot metal and clear rhinestones, **$85**.

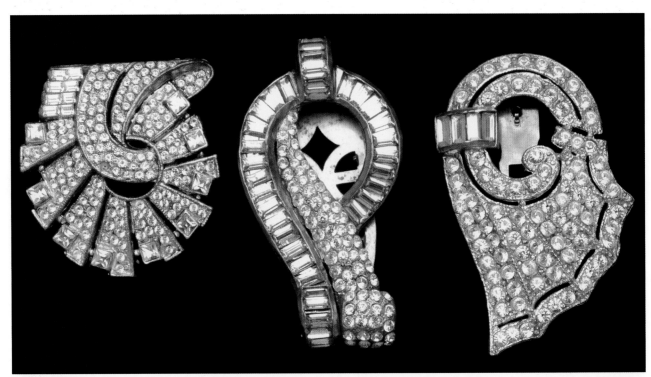

From left: Art Deco dress clip, pot metal and clear rhinestones, red cabochons, **$85**; Art Deco dress clip, pot metal and clear rhinestones, red cabochons, **$125**; Art Deco dress clip, pot metal and clear rhinestones, red cabochons, **$65**.

Dress clip, pot metal and clear rhinestones, **$165**.

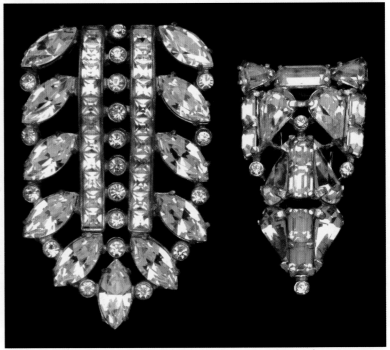

From left: Fenichel fur clip, pot metal and clear rhinestones, **$135**; Eisenberg (script E) fur clip, pot metal and clear rhinestones, **$185**.

From left: Art Deco dress clip, pot metal and clear rhinestones, **$95**; Art Deco dress clip, pot metal and clear rhinestones, **$145**; Art Deco dress clip, pot metal and clear rhinestones, **$110**.

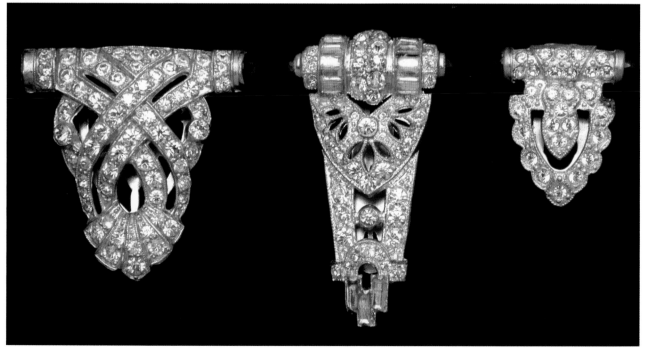

From left: Art Deco dress clip, pot metal and clear rhinestones, red cabochons, **$85**; Art Deco dress clip, pot metal and clear rhinestones, red cabochons, **$125**; Art Deco dress clip, pot metal and clear rhinestones, red cabochons, **$65**.

From left: floral design dress clip, pot metal and clear rhinestones, plastic flowers, **$68**; flower design dress clip, pot metal and clear rhinestones, **$98**; enameled flower dress clip, pot metal and clear rhinestones, **$78**.

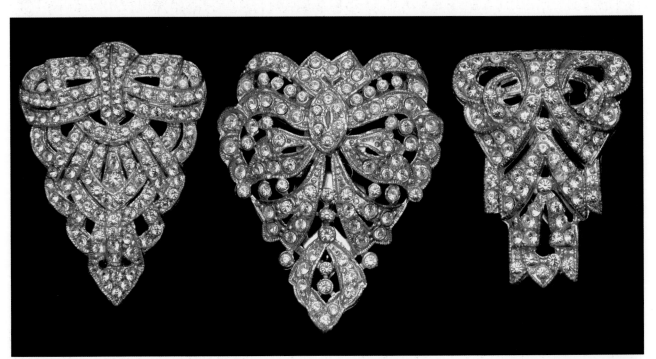

From left: Art Deco dress clip, pot metal and clear rhinestones, **$98**; bow design dress clip, pot metal and clear rhinestones, **$98**; Art Deco dress clip, pot metal and clear rhinestones, **$85**.

Pair of Art Deco dress clips, rhinestones and blue cabochons, **$125**.

From left: dress clip, pot metal and clear rhinestones, **$110**; flower dress clip, pot metal and clear and purple rhinestones, **$65**; grape design dress clip, pot metal and clear and blue rhinestones, **$82**.

Fur clip, rhodium and clear rhinestones, **$95**.

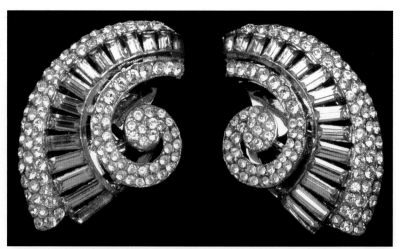

Pair of TKF dress clips, rhodium and clear rhinestones, **$125**.

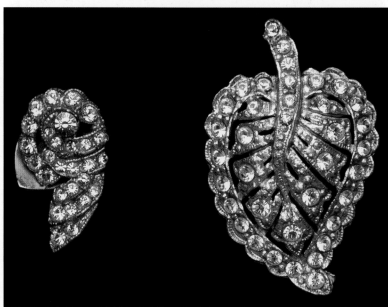

From left: leaf design dress clip, pot metal and clear rhinestones, **$48**; Art Deco dress clip, pot metal and clear rhinestones, **$32**; leaf design dress clip, pot metal and clear rhinestones, **$52**.

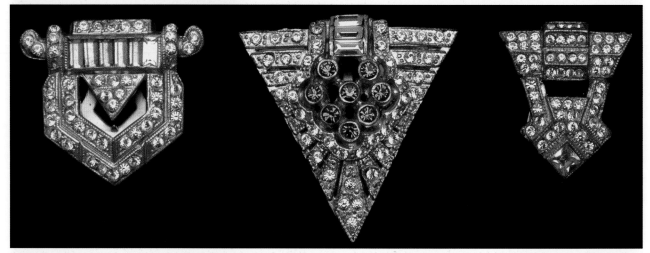

From left: Art Deco dress clip, pot metal and clear rhinestones, **$75**; Art Deco dress clip, pot metal and clear and blue rhinestones, **$72**; Art Deco dress clip, pot metal and clear rhinestones, **$85**.

From left: dress clip, pot metal and clear and faceted glass, **$65**; Art Deco dress clip, pot metal and clear and blue rhinestones, **$65**.

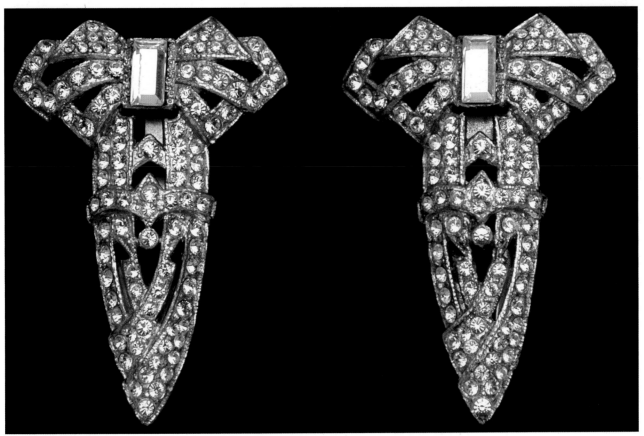

Pair of bow dress clips, pot metal and clear rhinestones, **$195**.

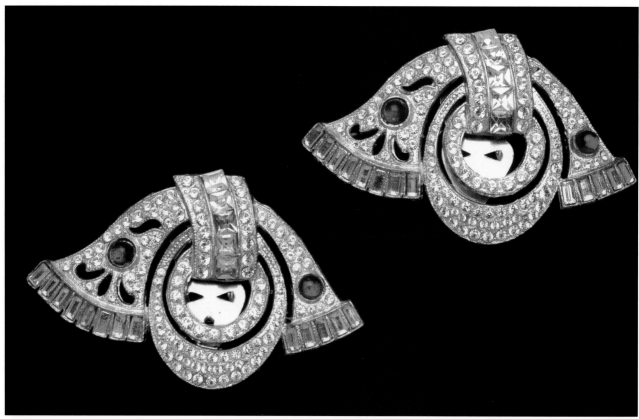

Pair of Art Deco dress clips, pot metal and clear rhinestones, green cabochons, **$195**.

From left: Coro dress-shaped dress clip, pot metal and clear rhinestones, **$145**; dress-shaped dress clip, pot metal and clear rhinestones, **$110**.

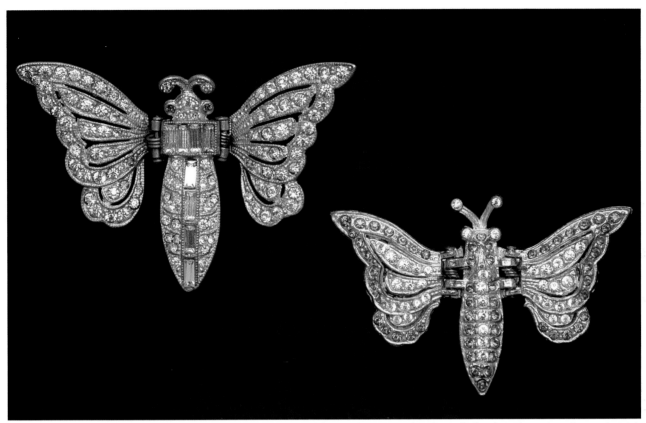

From left: butterfly fur clip with moving wings, pot metal and clear and green rhinestones, **$95**; butterfly fur clip with moving wings, pot metal and clear and blue rhinestones, **$88**.

Pair of leaf design dress clips, pot metal and clear rhinestones, **$165**.

Dress clip, pot metal and clear faceted glass, **$155**.

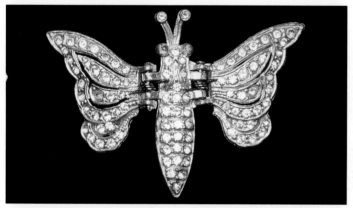

Butterfly clip, pot metal and clear and yellow rhinestones, **$85**.

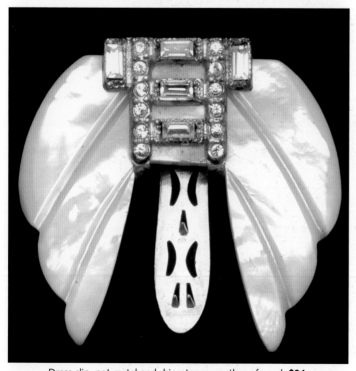

Dress clip, pot metal and rhinestones, mother of pearl, **$94**.

Dress clip, rhodium and clear rhinestones, **$195**.

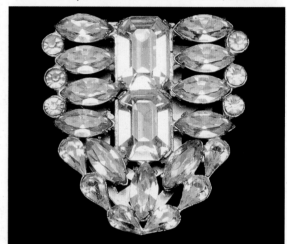

Dress clip, pot metal and clear rhinestones, **$75**.

Eisenberg Original fur clip, sterling and clear rhinestones, **$395**.

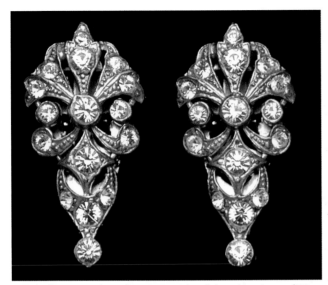

Pair of Art Deco dress clips, pot metal and clear rhinestones, **$88**.

Pair of Art Deco dress clips, pot metal and clear rhinestones, **$185**.

Pair of Art Deco dress clips, rhodium and clear rhinestones, **$145**.

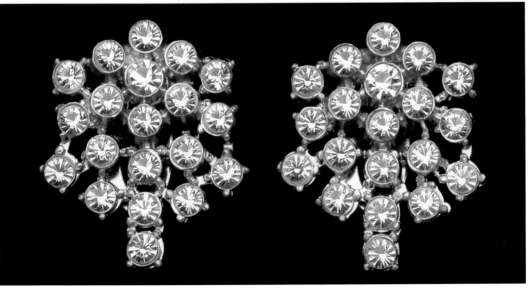

Pair of dress clips, pot metal and clear rhinestones, **$85**.

Art Deco dress clip, pot metal and clear rhinestones, **$195**.

Pair of bow dress clips, pot metal and clear rhinestones, **$55**.

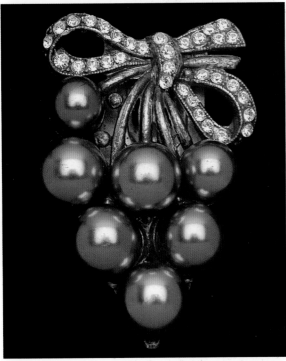

Grape dress clip, pot metal and clear rhinestones, faux pearls, **$95**.

Art Deco dress clip, pot metal and clear rhinestones, **$165**.

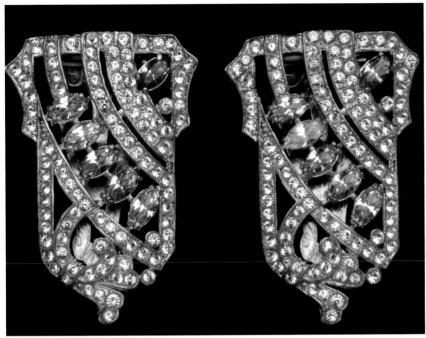

Pair of Art Deco dress clips, pot metal and clear rhinestones, **$145**.

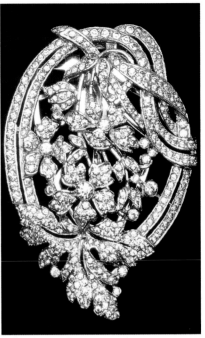

Trifari dress clip, rhodium and clear rhinestones, **$135**.

Woman's face fur clip, pot metal and clear, red, and green rhinestones, enameling, **$110**.

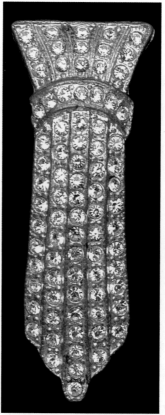

Flamingo fur clip, pot metal and red and clear rhinestones, enameling **$145**.

From left: Art Deco dress clip, pot metal and clear rhinestones, **$48**; Art Deco dress clip, pot metal and clear rhinestones, **$36**.

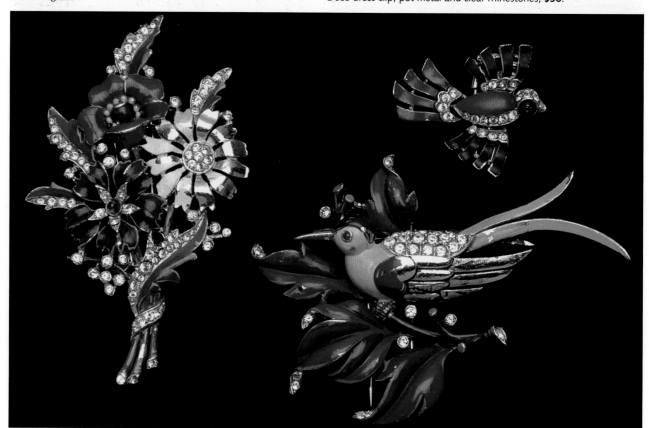

Clockwise from left: Trifari flower fur clip, enamel, rhodium and clear rhinestones, some wear to enameling, **$185**; Trifari bird fur clip, enamel, rhodium and clear rhinestones, **$155**; Trifari bird fur clip, enamel, rhodium and clear rhinestones, some wear to enameling, **$145**.

Left: Trifari fur clip, trembler with clear rhinestones, faux pearl, enameling, **$325**. Middle: Trifari fur clip, rhodium and clear rhinestones, enameling, **$195**. Right: Trifari fur clip, rhodium and clear rhinestones, enameling, **$155**.

Czechoslovakian fur clip, pot metal and red, green, blue, citrine rhinestones, **$65**.

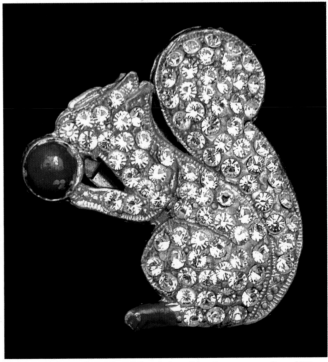

Squirrel dress clip, pot metal and clear rhinestones, enameling, **$85**.

191

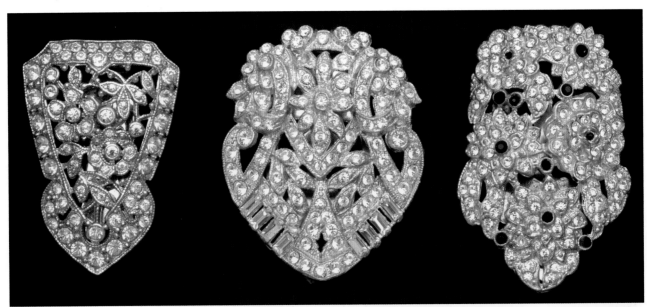

From left: floral design dress clip, pot metal and clear rhinestones and faux pearl, **$68**; floral design dress clip, pot metal and clear rhinestones, **$95**; floral design dress clip, pot metal and clear and black rhinestones, **$110**.

Art Deco dress clip, pot metal and clear rhinestones, **$45**.

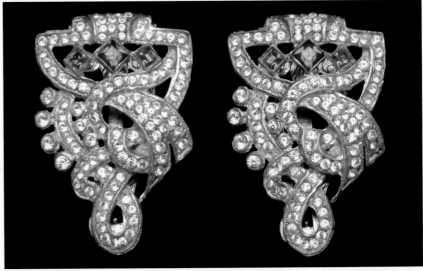

Pair of Art Deco dress clips, pot metal and clear and blue rhinestones, **$110**.

Art Deco dress clip, pot metal and clear rhinestones, **$42**.

Pair of Art Deco dress clips, pot metal and clear rhinestones, **$145**.

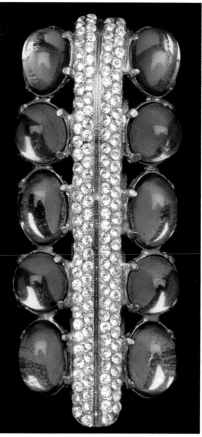

From left: Art Deco dress clip, pot metal and clear and blue rhinestones, **$95**; Art Deco dress clip, pot metal and clear and blue rhinestones, **$78**.

Art Deco dress clip, pot metal and clear rhinestones, blue glass cabochons, **$125**.

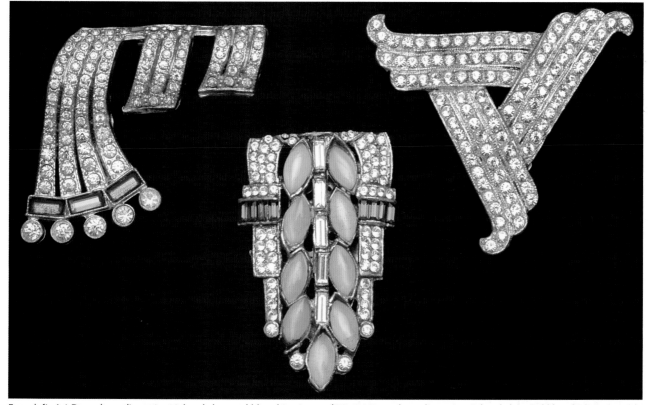

From left: Art Deco dress clip, pot metal and clear and blue rhinestones, **$78**; Art Deco dress clip, pot metal and clear and blue rhinestones, opalescent glass cabochons, **$95**; triangular-shaped dress clip, pot metal and clear rhinestones, **$98**.

From left: floral design dress clip, pot metal and clear rhinestones, **$90**; Art Deco dress clip, pot metal and clear rhinestones, **$95**; Art Deco dress clip, pot metal and clear rhinestones, **$48**.

Pair of Art Deco dress clips, pot metal and clear rhinestones, **$245**.

Art Deco dress clip, pot metal and clear rhinestones, **$125**.

Heart fur clip, pot metal and clear rhinestones, **$135**.

Art Deco dress clip, rhodium and clear rhinestones, **$185**.

Bird fur clip, pot metal and clear rhinestones, red and blue cabochons, faux pearl, enameling, some wear to enamel, **$165**.

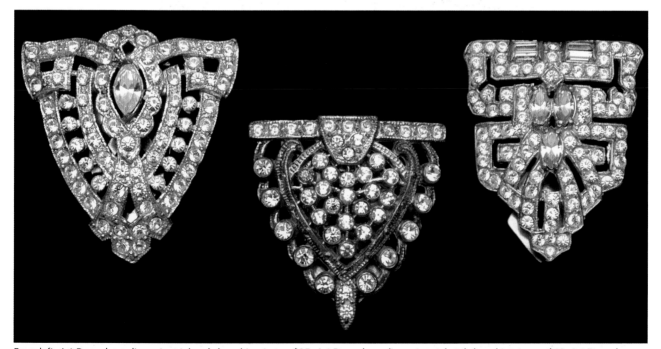

From left: Art Deco dress clip, pot metal and clear rhinestones, **$95**; Art Deco dress clip, pot metal and clear rhinestones, **$48**; Art Deco dress clip, pot metal and clear rhinestones, **$98**.

Dress clip, pot metal and blue rhinestones, **$65**.

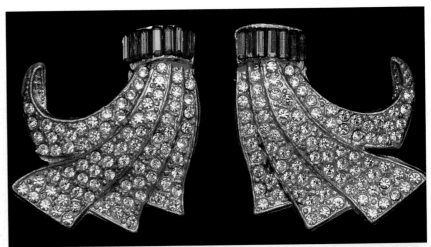

Pair of Art Deco dress clips, pot metal and blue and clear rhinestones, **$95**.

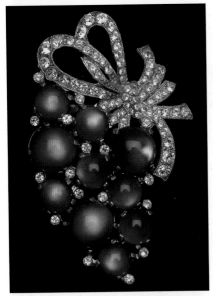

Grape fur clip, pot metal and clear rhinestones, blue glass cabochons, **$95**.

Pair of bow dress clips, pot metal and clear rhinestones, **$95**.

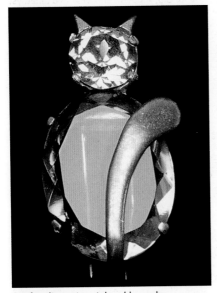

Cat fur clip, pot metal and lavender rhinestones, blue faceted glass, **$45**.

Pair of dress clips, pot metal and clear rhinestones, **$85**.

Pair of flower dress clips, pot metal and clear rhinestones, **$165**.

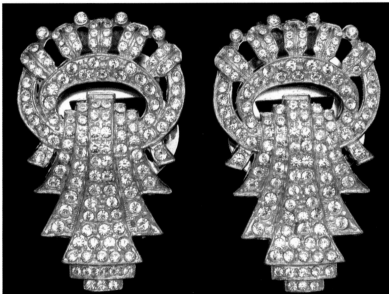

Pair of Art Deco dress clips, pot metal and clear rhinestones, **$185**.

Coro floral fur clip, rhodium and clear and amethyst rhinestones, enameling, **$95**.

Pair of Art Deco buckle dress clips, pot metal and clear rhinestones, **$85**.

Dress clip, pot metal and amethyst rhinestones, **$95**.

Flower fur clip, pot metal and clear rhinestones, pink glass cabochons, enameling, **$98**.

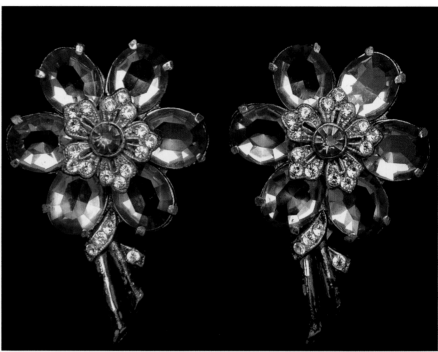

Pair of flower dress clips, pot metal and clear and blue rhinestones, blue faceted glass, enameling, some wear to enamel, **$145**.

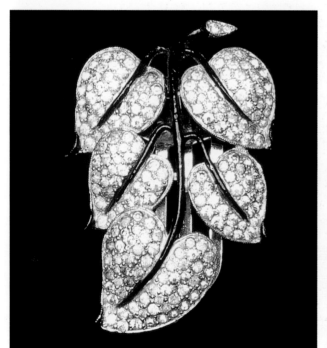

Trifari dress clip with clear rhinestones, enameling, **$165**.

Trifari floral fur clip, rhodium and clear rhinestones, **$175**.

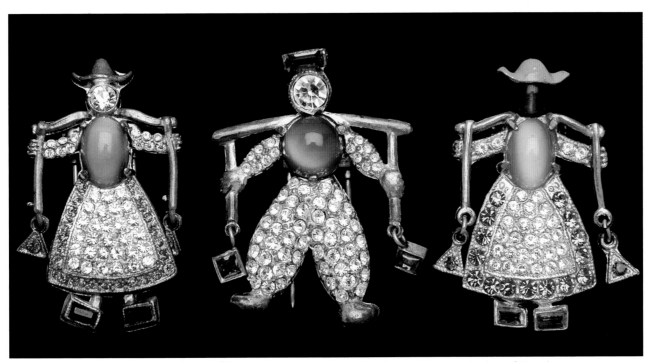

Figural fur clips, pot metal and clear, blue, green, and pink rhinestones, pink glass cabochons, **$85** each.

Grape design dress clip, pot metal, opalescent cabochons, enameling, **$85**.

Trifari floral design fur clip, rhodium and clear rhinestones, **$325**.

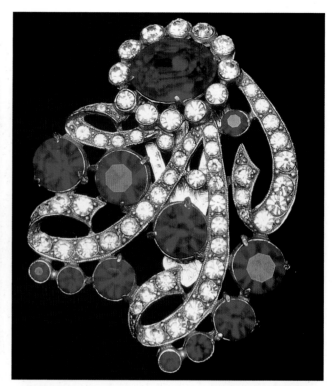

Staret dress clip, rhodium and clear and red rhinestones, **$245**.

Dress clip, rhodium and clear rhinestones, green glass cabochons, **$98**.

Flowers in vase dress clip, pot metal and clear rhinestones, molded glass, enameling, **$110**.

Trifari floral fur clip with clear rhinestones and enameling, **$325**.

Trifari fur clip with clear rhinestones and enameling, **$165**.

Flower dress clip, pot metal and clear and green rhinestones, enameling, **$65**.

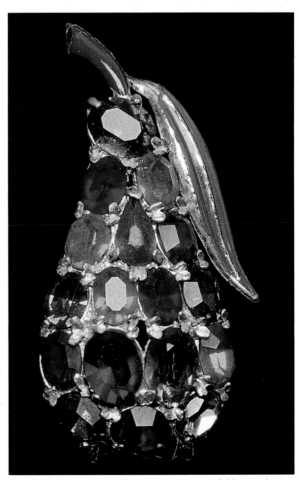

Pear fur clip, pot metal and amethyst, topaz, red, blue, and green rhinestones, enameling, **$65**.

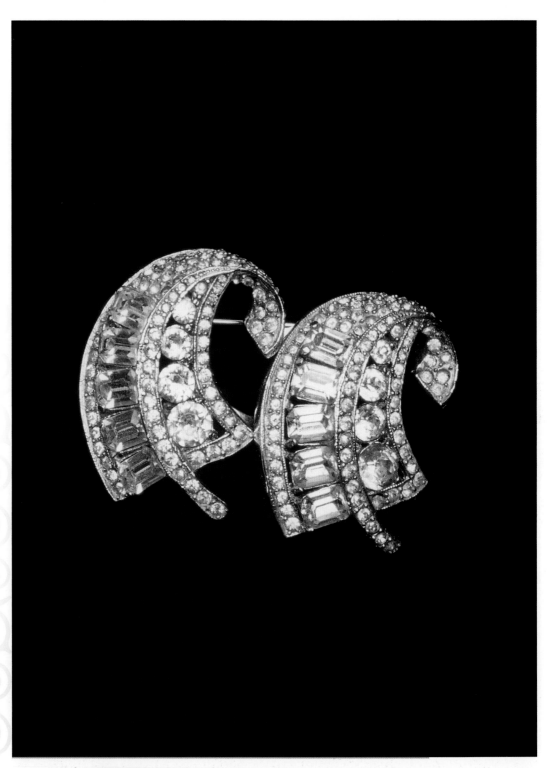

Duettes

From top: Art Deco duette, pot metal and clear and green rhinestones, **$145**; Art Deco duette, pot metal and clear rhinestones, **$165**.

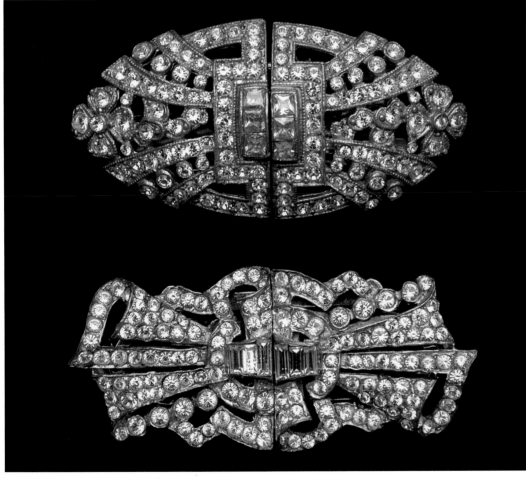

From top: duette, pot metal and clear rhinestones, **$145**; Art Deco clipmate, rhodium and clear rhinestones, **$165**.

Duette, pot metal and clear rhinestones, **$145**.

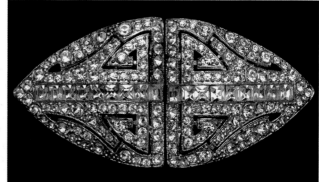

Coro Duette, pot metal and clear rhinestones, **$225**.

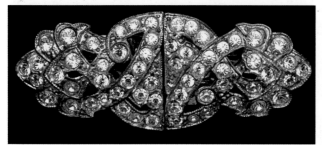

Coro Art Deco Duette, pot metal and clear rhinestones, **$225**.

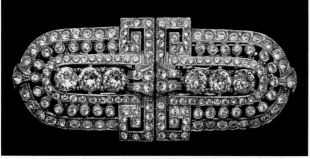

Art Deco duette, pot metal and clear rhinestones, **$225**.

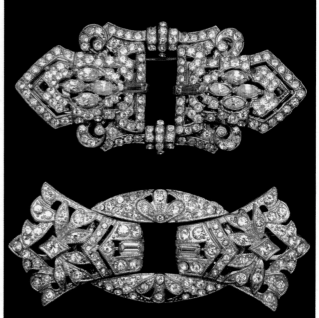

From top: Coro Art Deco Duette, pot metal and clear rhinestones, **$225**; Coro Art Deco Duette, pot metal and clear rhinestones, **$195**.

Coro Duette, pot metal and clear rhinestones, **$195**.

Clipmate, pot metal and clear rhinestones, **$165**.

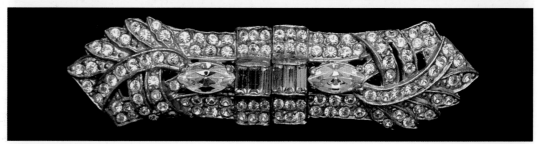

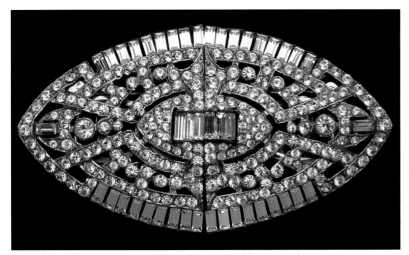

Coro Duette, pot metal and clear rhinestones, **$265**.

Coro Duette, pot metal and clear rhinestones, **$245**.

Coro Duette, pot metal and clear rhinestones, **$195**.

Coro Duette with clear rhinestones, **$345**.

Flower duette, pot metal and clear rhinestones, **$225**.

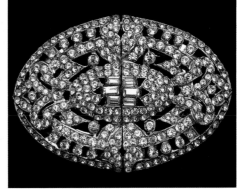

Coro Duette, rhodium and clear rhinestones, **$245**.

Duette, pot metal and clear and blue rhinestones, **$95**.

Clipmate, rhodium and clear rhinestones, **$155**.

Earrings

Art Deco earrings, sterling and clear rhinestones, red faceted glass, **$385**.

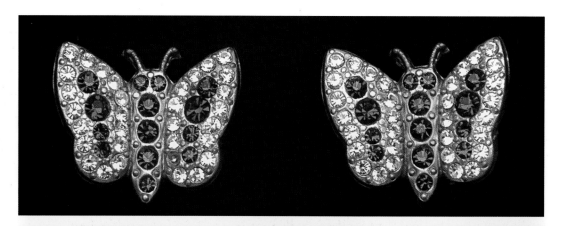

Butterfly earrings, pot metal and clear and green rhinestones, **$85**.

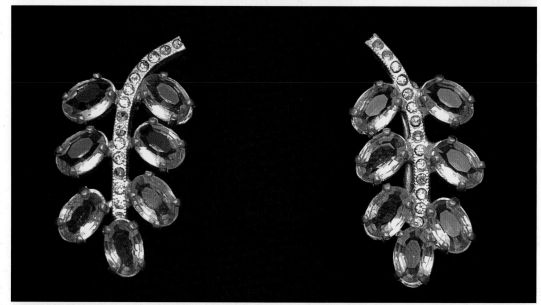

Czechoslovakian leaf earrings, pot metal and clear rhinestones, blue faceted glass, **$95**.

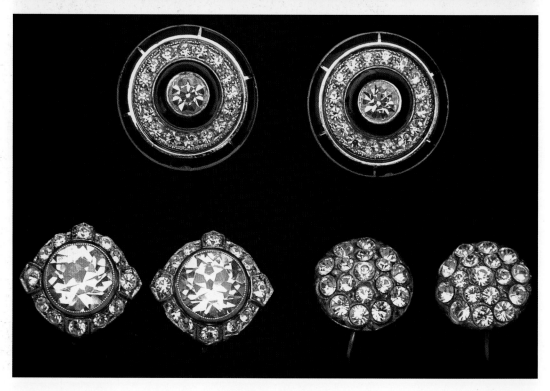

Clockwise from top: Art Deco earrings, rhodium and clear rhinestones, enameling, **$95**; earrings, pot metal and clear rhinestones, **$24**; Art Deco earrings, sterling and clear rhinestones, **$65**.

Art Deco earrings, pot metal and clear rhinestones, **$125**.

Art Deco earrings, pot metal and clear rhinestones, **$125**.

Czechoslovakian earrings, sterling and clear rhinestones, blue faceted glass, enameling, **$245**.

Art Deco earrings, pot metal and clear rhinestones, **$95**.

Earrings, sterling and blue rhinestones, **$45**.

From left: earrings, sterling and pink rhinestones, **$65**; earrings, sterling and blue faceted glass, **$45**.

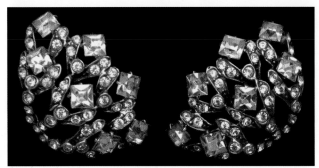

Crown earrings, sterling and clear rhinestones, **$95**.

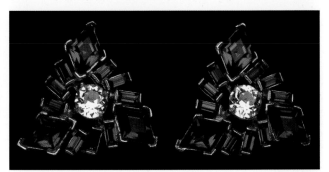

Earrings, pot metal and clear and green rhinestones, **$45**.

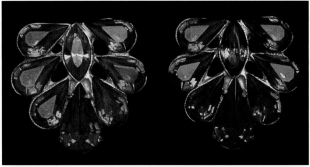

Earrings, pot metal and blue rhinestones, **$42**.

Earrings, pot metal and clear and blue rhinestones, **$42**.

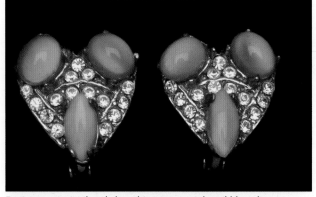

Earrings, pot metal and clear rhinestones, pink and blue glass cabochons, **$55**.

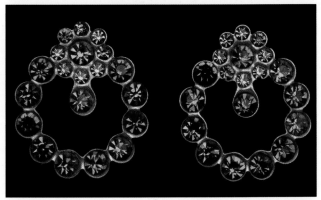

Art Deco earrings, pot metal and blue rhinestones, **$42**.

Art Deco earrings, pot metal and clear rhinestones, **$58**.

Art Deco earrings, pot metal and clear rhinestones, **$65**.

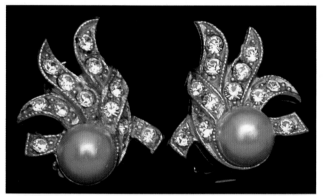

Earrings, pot metal and clear rhinestones, faux pearls, **$45**.

Art Deco earrings, rhodium and clear rhinestones, **$65**.

Art Deco earrings, sterling and pink rhinestones, **$125**.

Art Deco earrings, pot metal and clear and blue rhinestones, **$36**.

Flower earrings, pot metal and clear and pink rhinestones, **$28**.

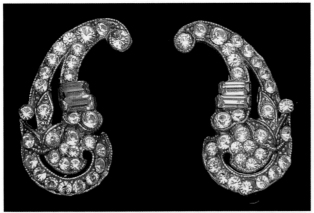

Art Deco earrings, pot metal and clear rhinestones, **$85**.

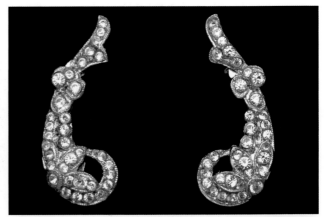

Art Deco earrings, rhodium and clear rhinestones, **$55**.

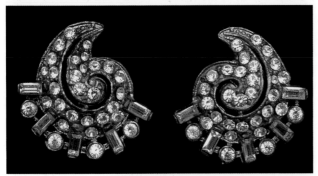

Art Deco earrings, pot metal and clear rhinestones, **$78**.

Art Deco earrings, pot metal and clear rhinestones, **$55**.

Leaf design earrings, pot metal and clear rhinestones, **$65**.

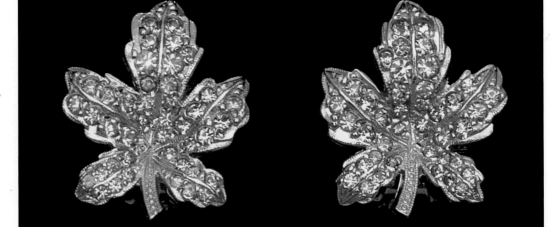

Jomaz earrings, rhodium and clear rhinestones, **$125**.

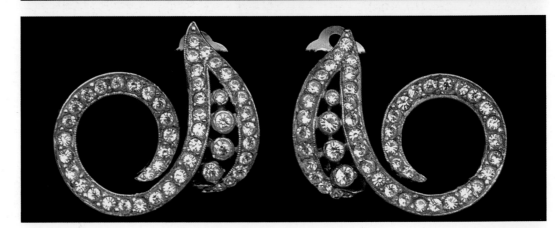

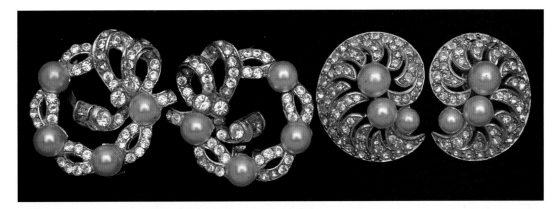

From left: Mazer earrings, pot metal and clear rhinestones, faux pearls, **$75**; Trifari earrings, rhodium and clear rhinestones, faux pearls, **$65**.

Earrings, pot metal and clear rhinestones, faux pearls, **$65**.

Art Deco earrings, pot metal and clear rhinestones, Bakelite, faux pearls, **$145**.

Art Deco earrings, pot metal and clear rhinestones, **$155**.

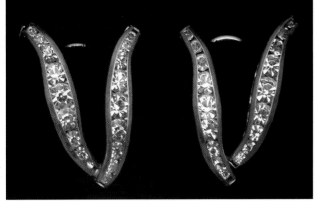

Art Deco earrings, pot metal and clear rhinestones, **$42**.

Art Deco earrings, pot metal and clear rhinestones, **$75**.

Czechoslovakian earrings, pot metal and clear rhinestones, clear faceted glass, glass beads, **$95**.

From left: bow earrings, pot metal and clear rhinestones, **$52**; bow earrings, pot metal and clear rhinestones, **$52**.

From left: earrings, pot metal and clear rhinestones, **$44**; earrings, pot metal and clear rhinestones, **$48**.

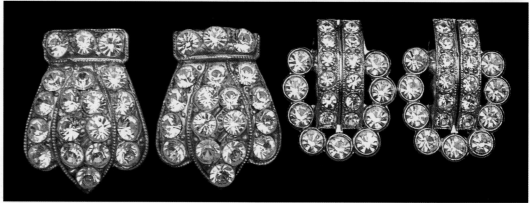

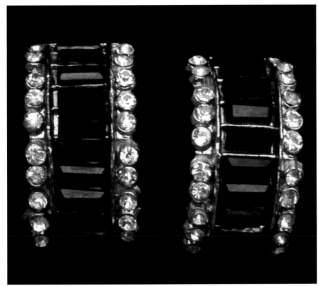

Hoop earrings, pot metal and clear and black rhinestones, **$48**.

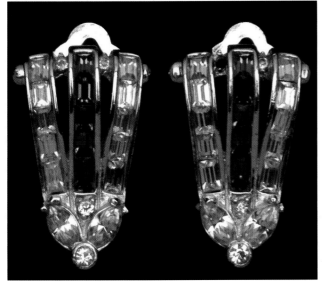

Pennino earrings, rhodium and clear and blue rhinestones, **$85**.

Art Deco earrings, pot metal and clear rhinestones, **$145**.

From left: Art Deco earrings, Claudette, pot metal and clear rhinestones, **$65**; Jomaz floral earrings, rhodium and clear rhinestones, **$95**.

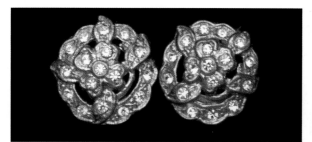

Flower design earrings, pot metal and clear rhinestones, **$58**.

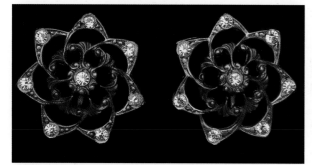

Earrings, pot metal and clear rhinestones, **$34**.

Czechoslovakian earrings, pot metal and clear rhinestones, molded glass, **$145**.

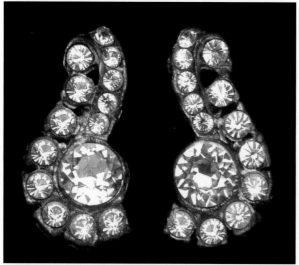

Art Deco earrings, pot metal and clear rhinestones, **$65**.

Art Deco earrings, pot metal and clear rhinestones, **$85**.

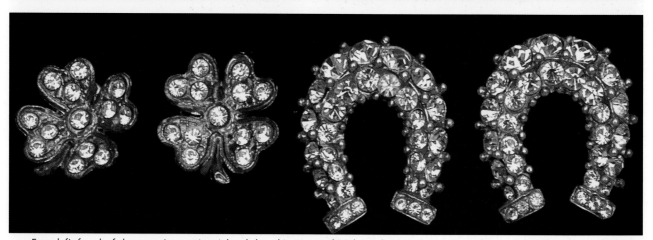

From left: four-leaf clover earrings, pot metal and clear rhinestones, **$36**; horseshoe earrings, B.B., sterling and clear rhinestones, **$66**.

Art Deco earrings, pot metal and clear rhinestones, **$95**.

Earrings, sterling and clear rhinestones, **$185**.

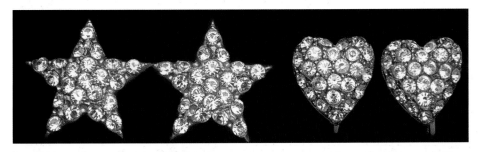

From left: star earrings, pot metal and clear rhinestones, **$45**; heart earrings, pot metal and clear rhinestones, **$45**.

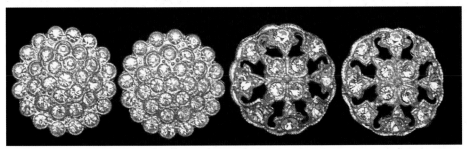

From left: earrings, pot metal and clear rhinestones, **$42**; earrings, pot metal and clear rhinestones, **$36**.

From left: Art Deco earrings, pot metal and clear rhinestones, **$35**; floral earrings, pot metal and clear rhinestones, **$55**.

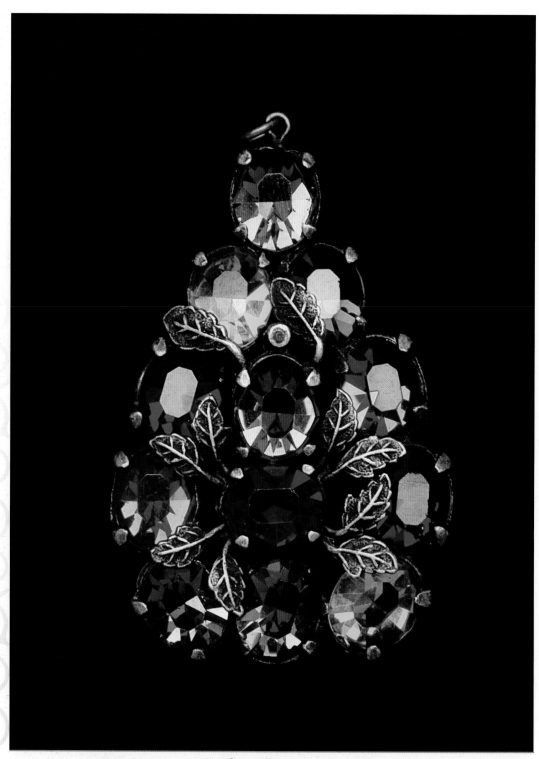

Necklaces
& Pendants

Necklace made of vintage buckle, pot metal and clear rhinestones, faceted contemporary amethyst and glass beads, **$625**.

Art Deco necklace, pot metal and rhinestones, **$95**.

Flower design necklace, pot metal and clear rhinestones, **$125**.

Art Deco necklace, rhodium and clear rhinestones, green faceted glass, **$295**.

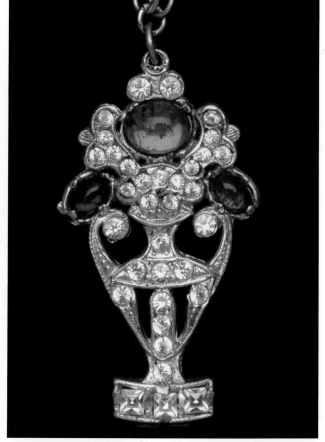

Flower basket design necklace, pot metal, rhinestones and green, red, and blue cabochons, **$125**.

Art Deco necklace,
pot metal and clear
rhinestones, **$125**.

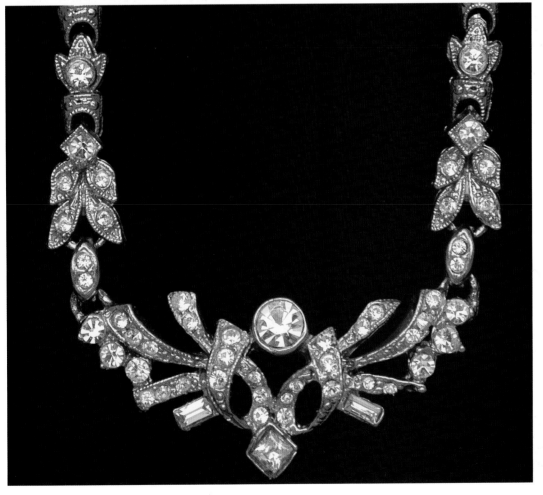

Necklace, pot
metal and clear
rhinestones, **$135**.

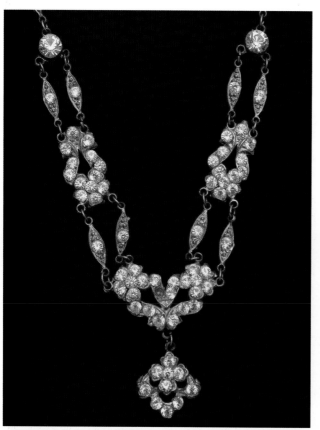

Art Deco necklace, pot metal and clear rhinestones, **$175**.

Bow design necklace, pot metal and clear rhinestones, **$185**.

Buckle necklace, pot metal and clear rhinestones, faux pearls, **$195**.

From top: floral design necklace, pot metal and clear rhinestones, **$125**; necklace, pot metal and clear rhinestones, **$98**.

Bow design necklace, Bakelite, and black and clear rhinestones, **$225**.

Trifari flower necklace, rhodium and clear rhinestones, **$185**.

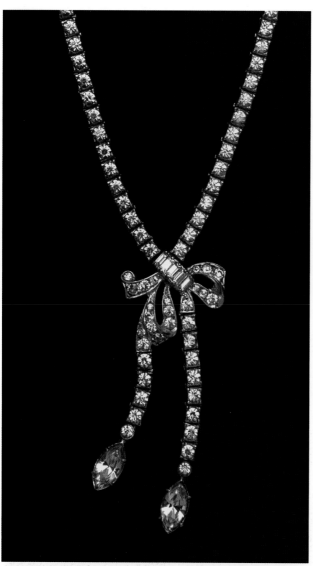

Sterling bow design necklace, rhinestones, **$345**.

Floral design necklace, pot metal and clear rhinestones, **$145**.

Choker made of vintage buckle, pot metal and clear rhinestones, vintage black glass beads, **$550**.

Leaf design necklace, pot metal and clear rhinestones, faux pearls, **$145**.

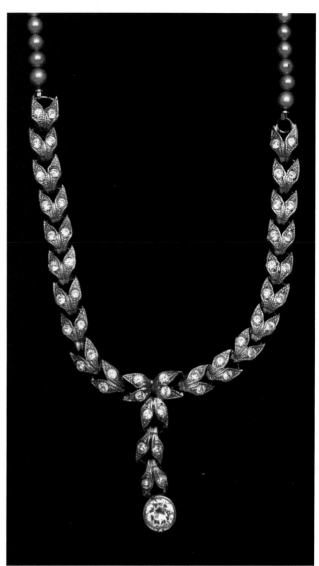

Leaf design necklace, pot metal and clear rhinestones, faux pearls, **$185**.

Three-strand faux pearl necklace made with vintage flower buckles, pot metal and clear rhinestones, **$450**.

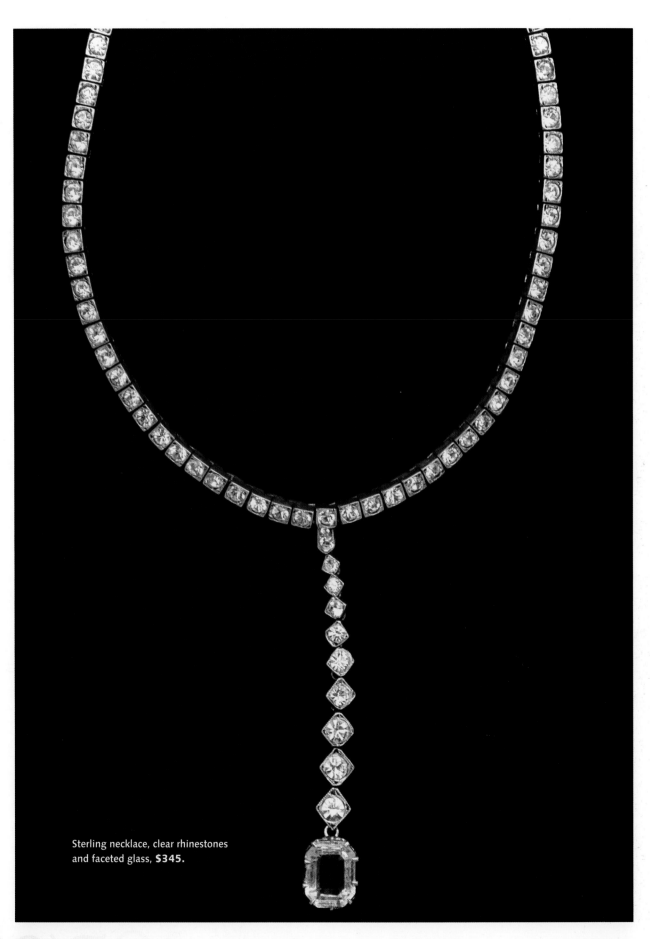

Sterling necklace, clear rhinestones and faceted glass, **$345.**

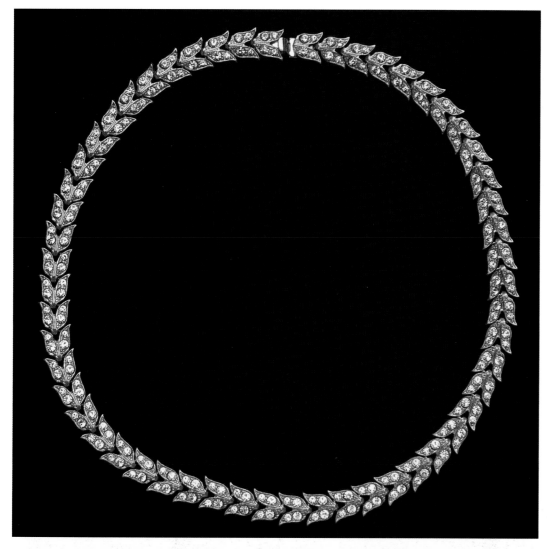

Leaf design
necklace,
rhodium and clear
rhinestones, **$165**.

Star design necklace,
pot metal and clear
rhinestones, **$185**.

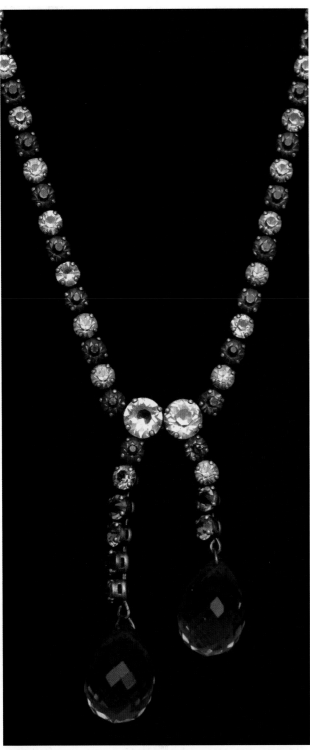

Czechoslovakian necklace, sterling and clear and blue faceted glass, **$245**.

Art Deco necklace, sterling and clear and blue rhinestones, blue faceted glass, missing a blue square cut rhinestone, **$395**.

Art Deco necklace, pot metal and clear and blue rhinestones, pink glass cabochons, **$185**.

Art Deco necklace, pot metal and clear rhinestones, green faceted glass, **$185**.

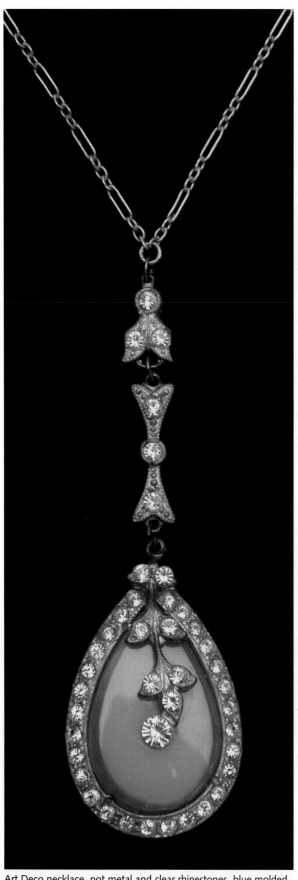

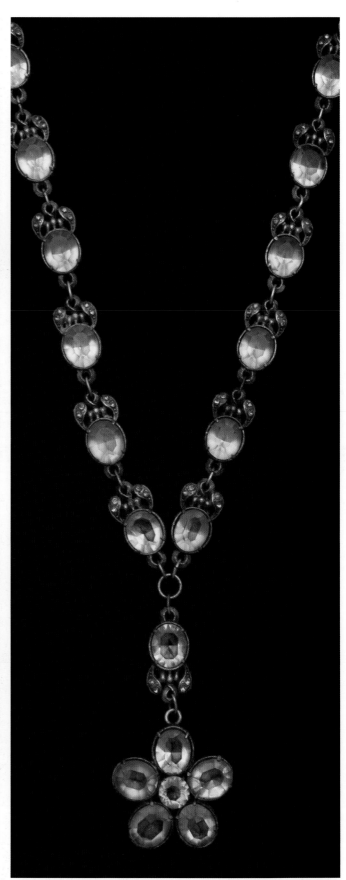

Art Deco necklace, pot metal and clear rhinestones, blue molded glass, **$155**.

Flower design necklace, pot metal and blue faceted glass, **$495**.

Czechoslovakian
necklace,
sterling and clear
rhinestones, clear
faceted glass, **$395**.

Necklace made from vintage flower pendant, pot metal and clear rhinestones, green faceted glass, vintage faux pearls, **$325**.

Art Deco necklace, pot metal and clear rhinestones, green faceted glass, **$195**.

Art Deco necklace, pot metal and clear and green rhinestones, green faceted glass, **$195**.

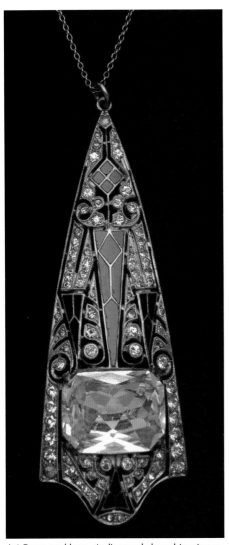

Art Deco necklace, sterling and clear rhinestones, clear faceted glass, enameling, **$495**.

Art Deco necklace, pot metal and clear rhinestones, faux pearls, **$295**.

Floral design necklace, pot metal and clear rhinestones, red faceted glass, **$245**.

Necklace made of vintage Art Deco buckle, pot metal and clear rhinestones, green glass cabochons, contemporary glass beads, **$650**.

Necklace made of vintage Art Deco buckle, pot metal and clear rhinestones, contemporary pink quartz beads, **$475**.

Alfred Philippe necklace, rhodium and clear and red rhinestones, **$750**.

Art Deco necklace, pot metal and clear rhinestones, **$180**.

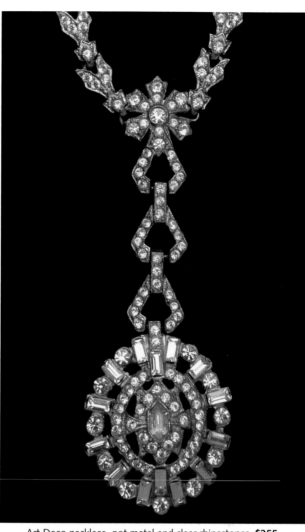

Art Deco necklace, pot metal and clear rhinestones, **$255**.

Pendant, pot metal and clear rhinestones on faux pearl necklace, **$195**.

Art Deco pendant on sterling chain, pot metal and clear rhinestones, blue faceted glass, **$245**.

Fruit design and enameled leaves necklace, pot metal and clear rhinestones, orange plastic cabochons, **$95**.

Art Deco pendant on chain, sterling and clear rhinestones, **$165**.

Art Deco pendant, pot metal and clear rhinestones, **$65**.

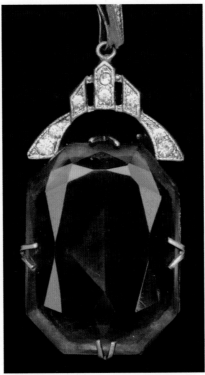

Art Deco pendant, pot metal and clear rhinestones, topaz-colored faceted glass, **$135**.

Pendant, pot metal and clear rhinestones, faux pearls, **$85**.

Pendant, pot metal with faceted glass stones in purple, citrine, blue, green, and red, **$95**.

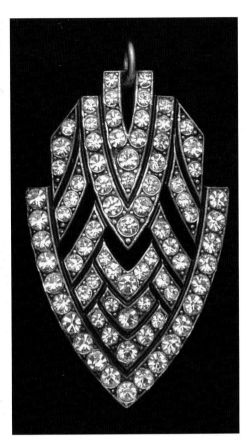

Art deco pendant, pot metal and rhinestones, **$145**.

Art Deco pendant, rhodium and green and clear rhinestones, **$155**.

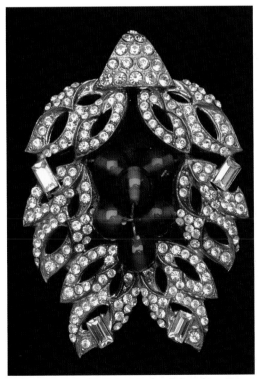

Grape design pendant, pot metal and clear rhinestones, purple glass beads, **$145**.

Leaf pendant, pot metal and clear rhinestones, **$115**.

Rings

Art Deco ring, pot metal and clear rhinestones, blue faceted glass, **$155**.

Art Deco ring, rhodium and clear rhinestones, **$145**.

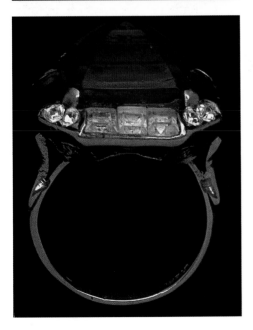

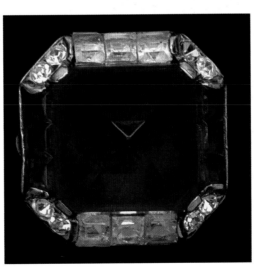

Art Deco ring, sterling and clear rhinestones, blue faceted glass, **$245**.

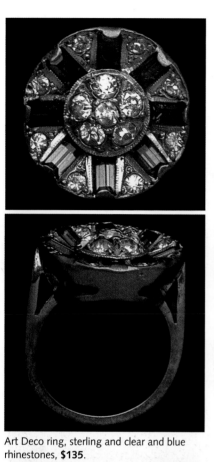

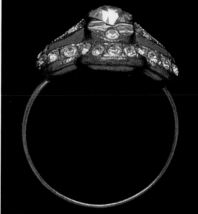

Art Deco ring, sterling and clear and blue rhinestones, **$135**.

Ring, pot metal and clear rhinestones, faux pearl, **$22**.

Art Deco ring, pot metal and clear rhinestones, **$135**.

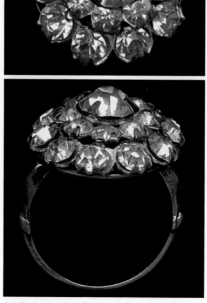

Ring, pot metal and clear rhinestones, **$85**.

Art Deco ring, sterling and clear rhinestones, **$65**.

Art Deco ring, pot metal and clear and blue rhinestones, **$85**.

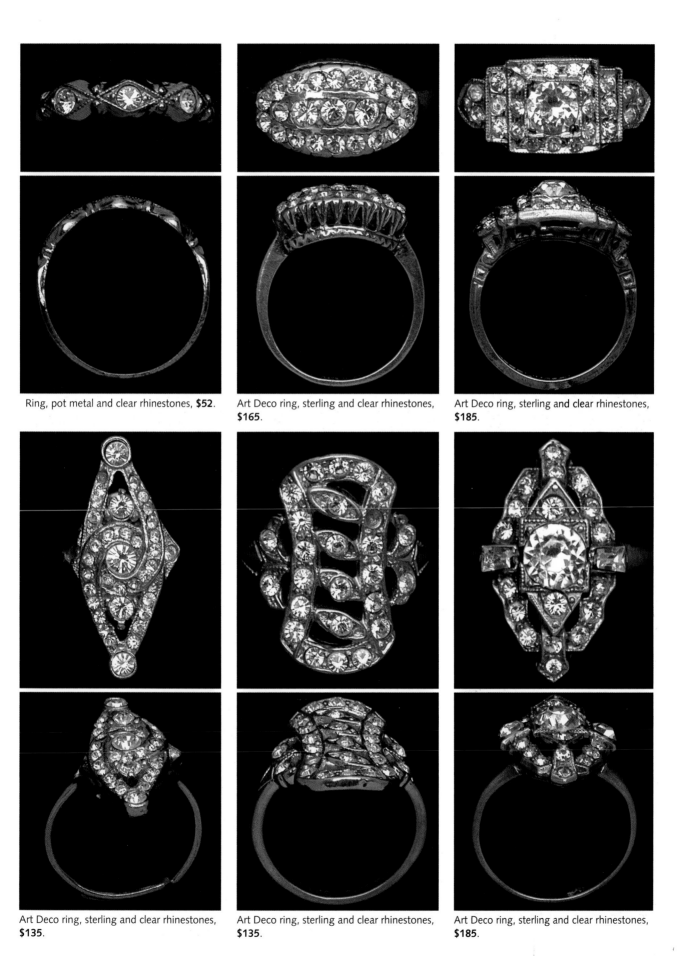

Ring, pot metal and clear rhinestones, **$52**.

Art Deco ring, sterling and clear rhinestones, **$165**.

Art Deco ring, sterling and clear rhinestones, **$185**.

Art Deco ring, sterling and clear rhinestones, **$135**.

Art Deco ring, sterling and clear rhinestones, **$135**.

Art Deco ring, sterling and clear rhinestones, **$185**.

Sets

Double bird Coro Duette and matching earrings, rhodium and clear rhinestones, enameling, **$425**.

Bird fur clip and matching earrings, pot metal and clear rhinestones, enameling, **$245**.

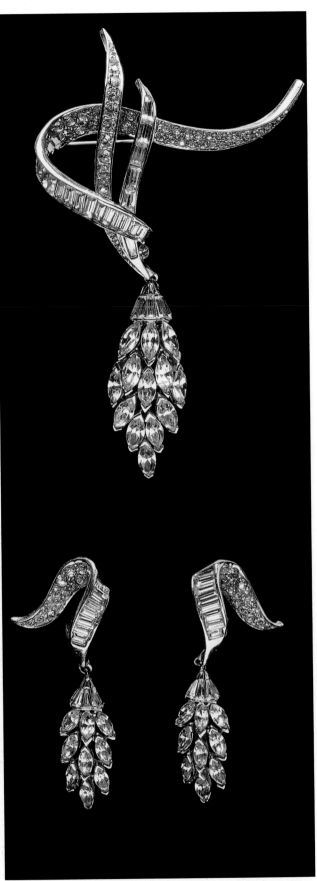

Art Deco brooch and earrings set, trembler brooch, pot metal and clear rhinestones, faux pearls, **$395**.

Boucher brooch and matching earrings, rhodium and clear rhinestones, **$245**.

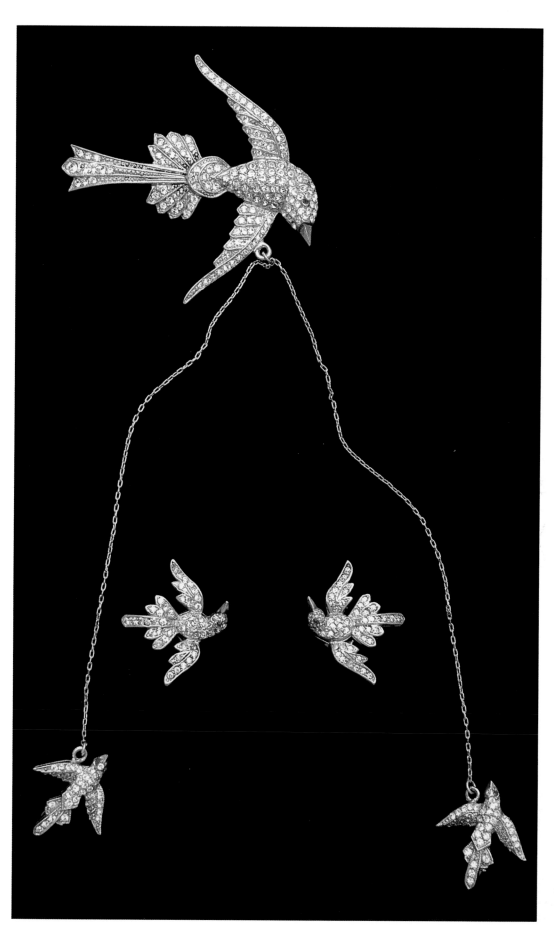

Trio of birds brooch
and matching
earrings, sterling
and clear and red
rhinestones, **$385**.

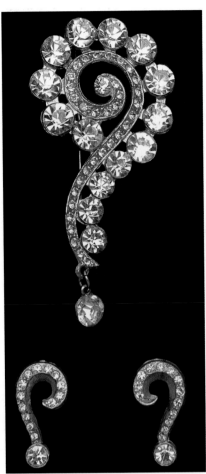

Question mark brooch and matching earrings, pot metal and clear rhinestones, **$145**.

Lily brooch and matching earrings, trembler, pot metal and clear rhinestones, **$255**.

Trifari brooch and earrings set, leaf design, rhodium and clear rhinestones, **$145**.

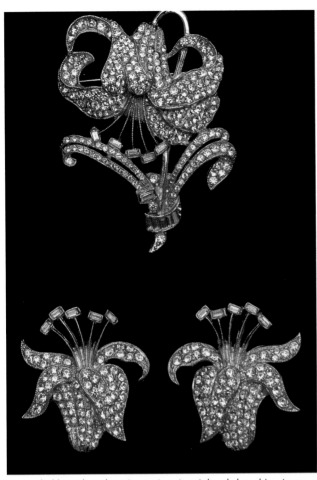

Ora orchid brooch and earrings set, pot metal and clear rhinestones, **$175**.

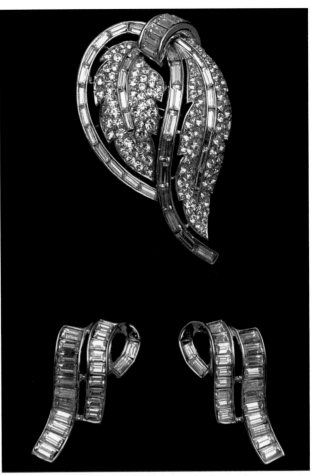

Trifari brooch and earrings set, leaf design, rhodium and clear rhinestones, **$195**.

Boucher fur clip and earrings set, pot metal and clear rhinestones, **$175**.

Bird pin and matching earrings, pot metal and clear and red rhinestones, blue glass cabochon, enameling, **$165**.

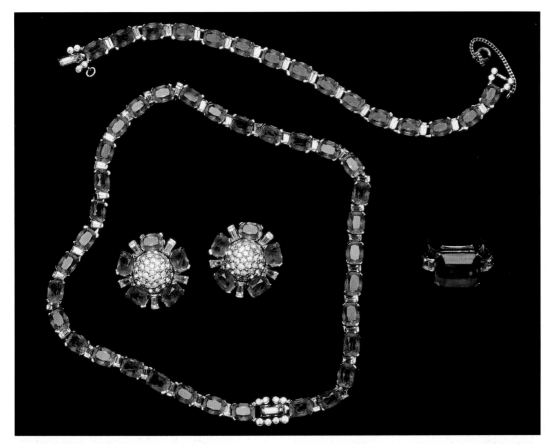

Jomaz necklace,
bracelet, earrings,
and ring, rhodium
and clear
rhinestones and
green faceted glass,
$345.

Reja matching
necklace, bracelet,
and earrings,
rhodium and clear
rhinestones, clear
faceted glass, **$325**.

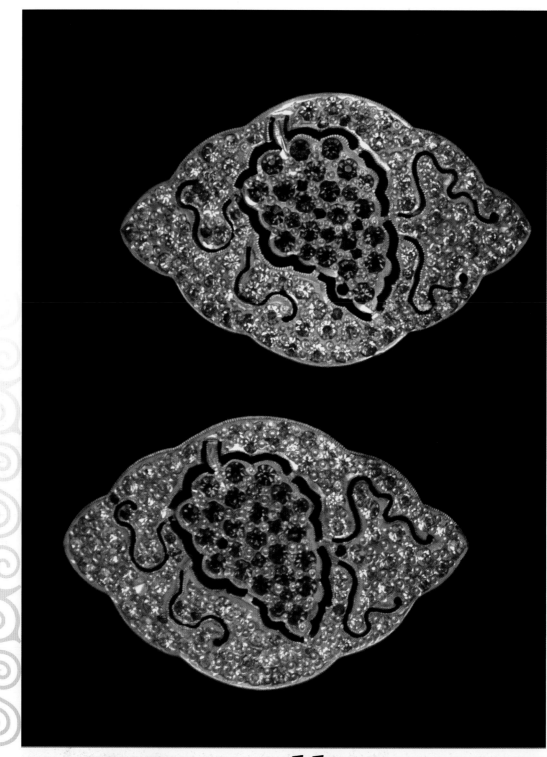

Miscellaneous

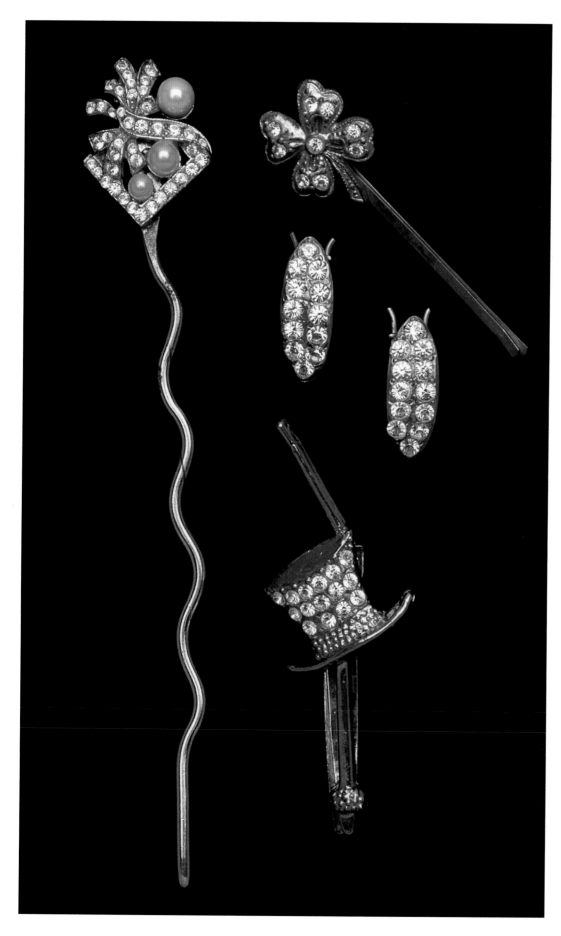

Left: chignon hairpin, pot metal and clear rhinestones, faux pearls, **$68**. Right, from top: four-leaf clover bobby pin, pot metal and clear rhinestones, **$42**; pair of barrettes, pot metal and clear rhinestones, **$38**; top hat hairclip, pot metal and clear rhinestones, **$45**.

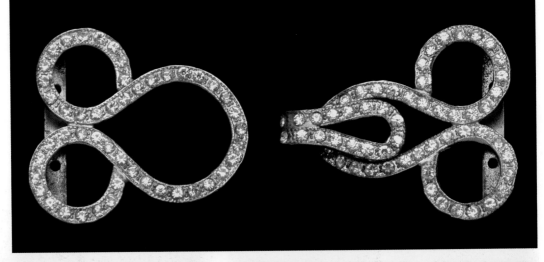

Art Deco buckle, pot metal and clear rhinestones, **$65**.

Buckle, pot metal and rhinestones, **$88**.

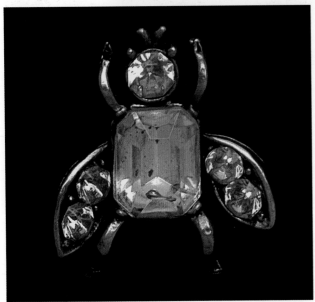

Bug button, pot metal and clear rhinestones, **$36**.

Button, pot metal and clear rhinestones, **$22**.

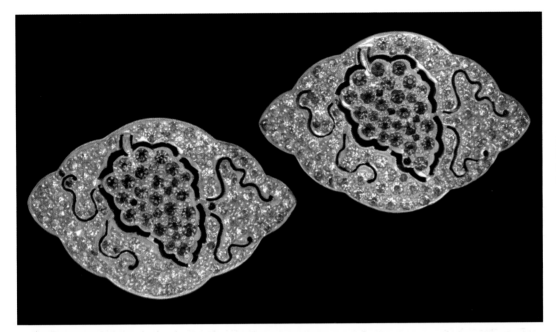

Pair of grape design buckles, rhodium and clear and purple rhinestones, **$110**.

Pair of rhinestone buttons, pot metal and clear rhinestones, green plastic stars, **$65**.

Pair of water bucket charms, pot metal and clear rhinestones, **$125**.

Buckle, pot metal and clear rhinestones, **$36**.

Orvin watch with pot metal and clear rhinestone band, **$245**.

Top: buckle, pot metal and clear rhinestones, **$55.**
Bottom: buckle, pot metal and clear rhinestones, **$75.**

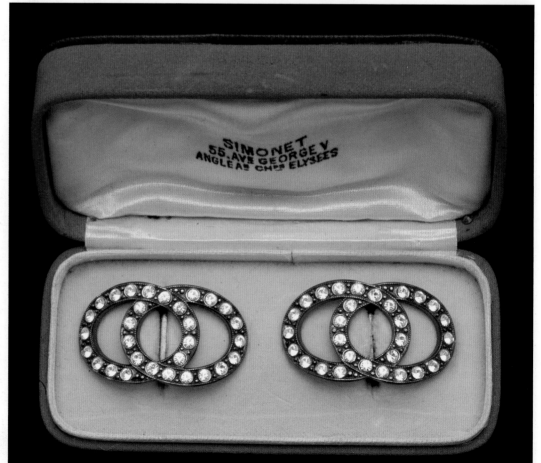

Pair of buckles in original presentation box, pot metal and clear rhinestones, **$95.**

Bibliography

Brown, Marcia. *Unsigned Beauties of Costume Jewelry*. Paducah, KY: Collector Books, 2000.

Brown, Marcia and Leigh Leshner. *Hidden Treasures: Rhinestone Jewelry*. Los Angeles, CA: Venture Entertainment Group, Inc., 1998.

Dolan, Maryanne. *Collecting Rhinestone & Colored Jewelry*. Florence, AL: Books Americana, 1993.

Leshner, Leigh. *Costume Jewelry: A Price and Identification Guide*. Iola, WI: Krause Publications, 2004.

Leshner, Leigh and Christie Romero. *Hidden Treasures: A Collector's Guide to Antique and Vintage Jewelry of the 19th and 20th Centuries*. Los Angeles, CA: Venture Entertainment Group, Inc., 1992.

Matlins, Antoinette. *Jewelry & Gems: The Buying Guide*. Woodstock, VT: Gemstone Press, 1997.

Romero, Christie. *Warman's Jewelry*. Iola, WI: Krause Publications, 2002.

Tucker, Andrew and Tamsin Kingswell. *Fashion: A Crash Course*. New York, NY: Watson-Guptill Publications, 2000.

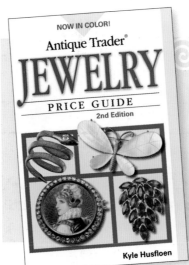

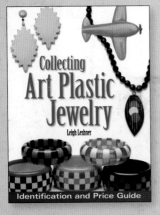